THE DANDELION HOUSE

&

SCENES FROM Love's Café

Lillenas Drama

THE DANDELION HOUSE

&

SCENES FROM Love's Café

by Nan Allen

Lillenas PUBLISHING COMPANY
KANSAS CITY, MO 64141

Printed in the United States of America

This is a royalty play. Permission to perform these works is granted upon the payment of a licensing fee of $15.00 for the first performance and $10.00 for each subsequent performance. Please use the form in the back of this book (page 71) to register your performance(s) and to submit the royalty payment. You may supply this information in the form of a letter.

The following should appear in your printed program:

"Produced by special arrangement with
Lillenas Publishing Co."

Lillenas Publishing Company
P.O. Box 419527
Kansas City, MO 64141

Cover Art by Mike Walsh

Dedication

The Dandelion House and *Scenes from Love's Café* are dedicated to "The Pew Prompters" at Judson Baptist Church, Nashville.

Contents

Preface

A special thanks to my family—Dennis, Mark, and Drew—for always encouraging me, for being willing to read manuscripts for the hundredth time, and for loving me unconditionally. And to my church family at Judson, I want to express my love and appreciation for letting me spread my wings and use my gifts.

The Dandelion House

Characters

GEORGE SAUNDERS: patriarch of the family and retired owner of Saunder's Gladiola Farm

LILLY SAUNDERS: George's wife, who feels personally responsible for everyone's health and happiness

PRESTON SAUNDERS: George and Lilly's oldest son; an A-type personality who runs the Gladiola Farm

ELIZABETH SAUNDERS: Preston's wife; a socialite who is image-conscious

CHASE (12) and CHELSEA (9): Preston and Elizabeth's children

CAMILLE: George and Lilly's daughter, a professional mother who has four children and one on the way, and she's into everything natural!

JERRY SAUNDERS: George and Lilly's youngest son; a free spirit and a teacher at a mission school in the Yukon Territory

LOUISE NASH: next-door neighbor

AUNT SAUCY BROWN: George's eccentric, overbearing sister

UNCLE HERMAN: Saucy's diminutive, henpecked husband

JAMES: a worker at the farm

ANDY: drugstore delivery boy

Setting

The living room is located at upstage center. There are two doors; one at up right (to outside the house), the other at up left (to the kitchen). Down left and right, in the premier performances, there were "wings," 8' x 8' extensions that jutted out at an angle from the front of the stage. The porch in Act I, Scene V is down right wing. The dining room in Act I, Scene III is down left. In the first staging there were two "balconies" at right and left of the stage. We used those for the bathroom in Act II, Scene I, and the boys' bedroom in Act I, Scene IV. Instead of utilizing balconies, these scenes could be placed at extreme right and left of the stage.

Props

I:1
knapsack
grocery sacks
miniature vacuum cleaner
extension cord

I:2
baseball bat
junk food/soft drinks

I:3
slices of pie
eating utensils
glasses of milk
plate of cookies

I:4
baby items
drugstore sack
clipboard/pencil

I:5
silver flatware

II:1
shaving items
hair brush, etc.
casserole dish
newspaper

II:2
pie
small basket/kernels of corn

ACT I

(It is Thanksgiving holiday, the Saunders' house. This is the first time in five years that the whole family has been together. JERRY *hasn't seen his parents in five years.* CAMILLE *has been giving birth for the last few years and hasn't been home much.* PRESTON, *the oldest, is running the family business and feels like the other siblings have deserted because they have gone on with their own lives. One at a time, the Saunders siblings discover that something's not quite right with Dad.)*

Scene 1

(The Saunders' living room: The room is clean but not very modern. There are lots of knickknacks on the tables, old photographs and portraits hanging on the walls, tired draperies and furniture. A bowl of plastic fruit sits in the middle of the dining room table.

(As the scene opens JERRY *enters wearing old ragged clothes. He carries a knapsack over one shoulder.)*

JERRY *("bursting" into the room through the outside door):* Ta da! *(Looks around)* Hey, everybody, Jerry's home! *(Steps further into room)* Hello. *(Crosses to kitchen)* Boy, it really smells like Thanksgiving in here. *(Crosses back to center, then to porch)* It's a little cool to be sitting out on the porch, don't you . . . think. *(Mimicking)* Well, welcome home, Gerald. So good to see you, my boy. Oh, Jerry, we've missed you so. *(Looks around, then crosses to dining room table, picking up plastic fruit)* Good ol' Mom. Still has that elegant eye for decorating. *(Notices clock)* Things haven't changed in five years. That old clock's still running 10 minutes slow. Kept telling Dad if he'd run it up 20 minutes, pretty soon it'd catch up with itself . . . *(Picking up a picture)* Oh wow. A picture of Jody. This must have been taken right before he . . . *(Offstage noise.* JERRY *hides behind door.)*

LILLY *(enters from outside with grocery sacks, talking to offstage):* Now, George, don't you try lifting those bags now, you hear. I'll be back . . .

(JERRY *steps out from behind the door and approaches* LILLY *from behind.)*

JERRY *(sticking his finger in her back):* Gimme all your dough . . .

LILLY *(drops sacks, raises hands):* Don't shoot. Silver's in the buffet. My good jewelry's in a can of tomatoes in the pantry.

JERRY: A *can* of tomatoes?

LILLY: Jerry? Is that you? *(Turns around)*

JERRY: Yeah, Mom, it's me.

LILLY *(grabbing his shoulders):* Jerry . . . Jerry . . . Jerry!

JERRY *(with same inflections):* Mom . . . Mom . . . Mom!

LILLY: You nearly scared me to death.

JERRY: I'm sorry.

LILLY: Oh, let me look at you. *(Holds him at arm's length)* Skin 'n' bones. You're not getting your nutrients. I can tell. Some of your food groups are lacking, aren't they?

JERRY: Now, Mom, don't start.

LILLY: What do you mean, don't start . . . I'm your mother . . .

JERRY *(interrupting):* Hey, where's Dad?

LILLY: Well, now, Jerry, your father is . . .

GEORGE *(entering from outside, doesn't notice* JERRY *at first):* Lil, where's that little bitty vacuum cleaner. Sack turned over, spilled a whole bag o' Stove Top Stuffing in the backseat . . . *(Sees* JERRY*)*

JERRY: Hi, Dad.

GEORGE *(after a pause, uncomfortably):* Hello, Gerald. Good to have you home.

JERRY: It's good to be home, Dad. You're looking, uh, real good. You've lost some weight, haven't you?

GEORGE: Well, Son, I haven't been feeling . . .

LILLY *(interrupting):* Your father didn't think you'd be home for Thanksgiving, Jerry. He's a little surprised.

JERRY: Actually, I'm a little surprised myself. The weather in the Yukon Territory is so unpredictable this time of year.

(Uncomfortable silence)

JERRY/GEORGE: So . . . how've you been? *(Both laugh.)*

JERRY/GEORGE: You go first. *(Both laugh.)*

JERRY/GEORGE: No . . . you . . . OK . . . I . . .

(They embrace.)

JERRY: Hello, Dad.

GEORGE: Hello, Son. Good to see you.

(Look at each other, smiling)

JERRY *(sigh):* Hey, let me clean up that mess in the backseat, huh? It's the least I can do. Where's the little vacuum cleaner, Mom?

LILLY: It's out in the kitchen, Jerry. On a shelf in the broom closet . . .

(JERRY *exits to the kitchen.)*

LILLY *(frantically):* Oh, George. What are we gonna tell the children? I mean, Jerry's here, Camille will be here tomorrow. Preston and his family will be here soon. And it's gonna come up. I just know it will.

GEORGE: Don't worry 'bout it, Lil. I'll handle it.

LILLY: But what are we gonna tell them, George?

(Enter JERRY *with vacuum cleaner.)*

JERRY: What are you gonna tell who what?

LILLY: Oh, nothing. What are we gonna tell . . . uh . . . the dry cleaners. . . . They . . . uh . . . pressed your father's lapels, and he doesn't like his lapels pressed, you know.

JERRY: Yeah, well . . . *(Looking a little perplexed)* I'll clean out the backseat for ya. *(Exits outside door)*

LILLY *(speaks toward the door):* Thank you, dear. *(To* GEORGE) Oh, George. That was close.

GEORGE: Lilly, why are you so worried about telling the children about my health? They're adults now. They can understand things like lab reports, prognosis—and cancer.

LILLY: Don't even say it, George! Don't say it!

(Enter JERRY.)

JERRY: Forgot the extension cord. Don't say what, Mom?

LILLY: Oh, uh . . . don't say . . . that the cleaners . . . uh, put too much starch in your father's shirts.

JERRY: Hmmmph. I'd switch dry cleaners if I were you, Dad.

GEORGE: Yeah, I plan to do that, Son.

(JERRY *exits to kitchen.)*

GEORGE: Now, Lilly. See what you've done? You've made me lie to my own son. I think we have to tell 'em.

LILLY: At least let's wait awhile. No need telling them now. It'll ruin the holiday.

GEORGE: Lilly, they've gotta know about my health. They have a right.

LILLY: Oh, George—I want this to be a good holiday.

GEORGE: So do I. But I want to treat this holiday—every holiday, for that matter—like it's my last.

(Enter JERRY *with extension cord.)*

JERRY: Your last what?

(LILLY *looks tense.)*

GEORGE: My . . . uh . . . last time to use that dry cleaners. *(Looks at* LILLY *and shakes his head)*

JERRY: Yeah, I thought you already decided that.

LILLY: Yes, dear. That's right. Your father just forgot, that's all. *(To* JERRY) Now, Jerry. Sit down . . . tell us about your work.

JERRY: I haven't cleaned out the backseat yet.

LILLY: Oh, that can wait. Let's talk.

GEORGE: Yes, Gerald. We've got some important things to talk about.

(LILLY *gives* GEORGE *a frantic look.)*

LILLY: How's your work going in the Yukon Territory? *(Proudly)* My son, the missionary.

JERRY: I'm not really a missionary, Mom. I just teach in a mission school.

GEORGE: Your mother likes to brag about you to the Women's Missionary Society.

JERRY: Like I've been telling you in my letters, it's great! The missionary school at Whitehorse is incredible. They're fully equipped now with books and supplies and computers. And the kids, Mom, the kids are awesome. It's a lot of work, but it's so rewarding.

GEORGE: I know you've been very busy.

JERRY: That's why I haven't been home for a while . . .

LILLY: Five years, four months.

JERRY: And the Bible studies we're having in some of the parents' homes—well, it's really growing. Since I've been there . . .

LILLY: For *five years* and *four months* . . .

GEORGE *(chiding):* Lil!

JERRY: It's OK, Dad. Mom, I should have come home more often. But it's so far away, and the weeks just kind of melt into months, and the months into years—I know, five years!

LILLY: And four months.

JERRY: Well, I think you'd be proud of the work I'm doing.

LILLY: Oh, we are, Jerry, we are. We just miss you, that's all.

JERRY: And I miss you too. Really. Sometimes I miss you so bad it hurts.

GEORGE: It hurts us too.

LILLY: We're glad you're home. This is one Thanksgiving that we'll never forget. Everybody'll be here.

JERRY: Yeah? Preston and Elizabeth and their two children? Camille and her—how many kids does she have now?

LILLY: Three . . . no four. Forgot about little Taylor. And there's one on the way. You did know that, didn't you? It's a good thing her husband, Chuck, is in construction. He just keeps building onto that house of theirs every time a new baby comes along.

GEORGE *(annoyed):* Their house looks like an EconoLodge. Has this bright aqua roof. You can see the thing all the way from the Interstate.

JERRY *(laughing):* Oh, that's great. That's just like Camille.

GEORGE: It's embarrassing, that's what it is . . .

JERRY: I guess she's still into natural everything . . . childbirth, organic gardening . . . and recycling? She still making all their clothes from flour sacks?

LILLY: Yes. Camille—she's always been a little dramatic.

GEORGE *(grumbling, under his breath):* I put her through college so she can live like a hippie. Raised her under the same roof with Preston and you. *(Looks at* JERRY) Never mind.

LILLY: Now, George.

(GEORGE *rolls his eyes.)*

JERRY *(uncomfortably):* Speaking of Preston, how *is* my big brother?

LILLY: Oh, he's doing just fine. His and Elizabeth's children are nearly grown. Chase is 12 and Chelsea's 9.

GEORGE: He's doing a marvelous job running the business for me. In fact, Preston's better at it than I ever was.

LILLY: Now, George, that's not true.

GEORGE: Oh, I knew how to grow gladiolas—but running a gladiola farm. Well, that's another thing. No, Preston's much better at managing. He's really turned a profit.

LILLY: 'Course, Elizabeth spends every dime Preston makes. At the salon one day, the country club the next. And when she's not there, she's at the mall.

GEORGE: Now, Lillian. Elizabeth is a fine daughter-in-law. She comes from a good Christian family. She and Preston are leaders in the church. Preston's stable . . . dependable . . .

(LILLY *shakes her head and sighs.)*

JERRY: Sounds like old times, all right. Everybody having a different opinion. So, then, how are you two getting along? Everything OK health-wise?

LILLY *(quickly changing the subject):* Oh my, look at the time. I need to get those groceries put up and start dinner.

GEORGE: Yeah, I uh, need to call the cleaners.

LILLY: Jerry, why don't you make yourself at home?

GEORGE: Sure, unpack and relax.

(As LILLY *and* GEORGE *exit to kitchen, a silent argument erupts between them.)*

JERRY *(looking somewhat perplexed):* So, welcome home, Jerry!

(Blackout)

Scene 2

(Two hours later. JERRY *is discovered asleep on the couch. There is a knock at the outside door.* JERRY *does not respond. Another knock.* JERRY *awakes.)*

JERRY: Mom, somebody's at the door.

(Another knock)

JERRY: Mom . . . Dad . . . door!

(Another knock)

JERRY *(sits up; has a conversation with himself):* Jerry, will you get that? Sure, I'll get it! Thanks! No problem.

(JERRY *opens door.* LOUISE *is standing there with a baseball bat raised above her head.)*

LOUISE: Hold it! Neighborhood Watch! I've just called 911 and you are dead meat, buster.

JERRY: Wait! No! Mrs. Nash. It's me, Jerry.

LOUISE *(suspiciously):* Jerry? Jerry who?

JERRY: Jerry Saunders. Don't you recognize me? I used to live here.

LOUISE: How do I know that you're really Jerry Saunders?

JERRY: Well, uh . . . uh . . . OK. You used to have a parakeet named Skipper who could whistle the "Gilligan's Island" theme song. Doesn't that prove I'm Jerry Saunders?

LOUISE: No, that's a matter of public record. Anybody could have found that out.

JERRY: Public record? A parakeet? You're kidding. (LOUISE *raises the bat higher.)* OK . . . OK . . . I put Salvo tablets in the little angel fountain on your front lawn. It foamed for days.

LOUISE *(lowers the bat):* Jerry, it was *you* who did that?

JERRY: Yes, ma'am, it was me.

LOUISE *(embracing him):* Jerry . . . Jerry . . . Jerry!

JERRY: Mrs. Nash! Mrs. Nash! Mrs. Nash! Whew, you had me scared there for a minute.

LOUISE: Well, you can't be too careful these days. I saw a strange automobile in the driveway, and I knew that George and Lilly had gone to the Wal-Mart. They go to Wal-Mart every Wednesday, you know. That's when they put Dr. Pepper on sale.

JERRY: Oh, I understand. It's OK. *(Pointing to baseball bat)* Hey, Mrs. Nash, is that the Louisville Slugger we used to use to play ball in your backyard?

LOUISE: Sure is. I sleep with it under my pillow every night.

JERRY: What does Mr. Nash think of that?

LOUISE: Oh, Jerry, Mr. Nash passed on two years ago.

JERRY: I didn't know Mr. Nash had died.

LOUISE: No, no. He didn't die. He just passed on—to Albany, last I heard.

JERRY: I'm really sorry to hear that. I didn't know.

LOUISE: Oh, let's don't talk about that. I want to hear about you, Jerry. It's been a long time since I've seen you. I know your folks are really glad you're home—under the circumstances.

JERRY: The circumstances?

LOUISE: You know, on account of your daddy's condition.

JERRY: What condition? What are you talking about, Mrs. Nash?

LOUISE *(embarrassed):* Oh, I've said too much already. *(Trying to hurry out)* My goodness, I need to get home and start supper for Mr. Nash. *(She desperately tries to exit before she says more.)*

JERRY: I thought you said Mr. Nash left you two years ago.

LOUISE: Oh, well, I did. But he might come home one day. And if he does, I'd like to have supper ready for him. Bye! *(Exits hurriedly)*

(JERRY *pauses and stares at the door for a moment.)*

JERRY: Mom! Dad! I need to talk to you. *(Crosses toward kitchen)* Come out, come out wherever you are. *(Exits into kitchen)*

(Enter CHASE *and* CHELSEA *from outside, arguing.)*

CHELSEA: Grandma said I could . . .

CHASE: Did not.

CHELSEA: Did too.

CHASE: Chelsea, Grandma didn't say you could pick *any* flowers out of her greenhouse, just the ones she doesn't want.

CHELSEA: Chase, Grandma said . . . *(Enter* JERRY *from the kitchen; he's carrying junk food and a Coke.* CHELSEA *stops dead in her tracks.)* Who are you?

JERRY: Who wants to know?

CHELSEA: I do . . .

JERRY: Wait a minute. You're not Chelsea . . . and Chase!

CHASE: Who wants to know?

JERRY: It's me—Uncle Jerry.

CHELSEA: Uncle Jerry! *(Embraces Jerry)*

CHASE: My dad said you were at the North Pole . . . living on an iceberg . . . eating blubber!

JERRY *(somewhat sarcastically):* Ah, that dear brother of mine. What a kidder. Actually, Chase, I teach school in the Yukon.

CHELSEA: Wow! The Yukon! Did you hear that, Chase? Uncle Jerry teaches in the Yukon! *(Beat)* Where's the *Yukon?*

JERRY: It's up in the northwest corner of Canada. It's very cold there.

CHASE: Sounds boring.

JERRY: Not really. We see elk and caribou and reindeer . . .

CHELSEA: Reindeer? Do you see Santa Claus too?

JERRY: Uh . . . no . . . Chelsea. We don't see Santa Claus.

(CHELSEA *looks disappointed.)*

JERRY: Say, where are your parents? Aren't they with you?

CHASE: Dad's working and Mom's parking the B-mer.

JERRY: Parking the B-mer?

CHASE: Yeah, she won't park it on this street. Too many trees with sap and pollen. She parks two blocks away in what she calls "a more suitable environment for the machine."

JERRY: Oh, is that right?

(Enter ELIZABETH *from outside.)*

ELIZABETH: Kids, I hope you wiped your feet. Grandma's cheap carpet doesn't repel stains like ours. *(Sees* JERRY) Oh . . . who are you? *(Draws* CHELSEA *near, fearfully as though she's afraid of* JERRY.)

JERRY: Elizabeth. It's me, Jerry.

ELIZABETH *(carefully looks at* JERRY, *still not sure):* Of course, Jerry. (JERRY *extends a handshake, which* ELIZABETH *reluctantly accepts.)* Good to see you. It's been awhile.

JERRY: Yes, it has. You're looking great, Elizabeth!

ELIZABETH: Oh, well, I just threw something on. This old thing, I'll probably throw it out at the next clothes drive.

(Enter GEORGE *and* LILLY *from outside.)*

GEORGE: Elizabeth. Kids. Hi . . .

LILLY *(to* CHELSEA): Oh, there's my little buttercup. Give Grandma some sugar. (CHELSEA *goes to* LILLY *and embraces her.)*

CHELSEA: Grandma, you said I could pick flowers out of your greenhouse, didn't you?

LILLY: Well, my goodness, my extremely rare hybrid Grand Pink. Well, oh, sure, sweetheart. You can pick Grandma's flowers anytime you want.

(CHELSEA *looks at* CHASE *and sticks out her tongue.)*

ELIZABETH: Actually, Lillian, we just stopped by to see if we could bring something for Thanksgiving dinner tomorrow. I would just be delighted.

GEORGE: That's very generous of you, Elizabeth.

ELIZABETH: Oh, well, I'll just have my cook, Beatrice, whip something up. I'm sure it'll be good. It always is.

LILLY *(a little miffed):* No thank you, Elizabeth. I think I can handle one family meal without Beatrice's help.

(GEORGE *looks annoyed at* LILLY.)

ELIZABETH: Well, all right. Of course, if you change your mind, you know where to reach me.

LILLY: The country club? Or the salon?

ELIZABETH *(laughing):* My service knows where to find me at all times.

LILLY: I'll bet!

GEORGE *(trying to rescue the situation):* So, how's Preston doing today?

ELIZABETH: Oh, you know—he's, uh busy. Very busy. *(Sighs)* Well, I just dropped by. I'll walk over and get the car. Ready to go, kids?

JERRY: It's good to see you, Elizabeth.

ELIZABETH: Oh, yes, I'm sure.

JERRY: Guess we'll see you tomorrow around the table, huh?

ELIZABETH: Yes, I suppose so.

CHASE and CHELSEA: Good-bye, Grandma . . . Grandpa.

CHELSEA: Good-bye, Uncle Jerry.

JERRY: Bye, Chelsea . . . Chase.

(ELIZABETH, CHELSEA, *and* CHASE *exit to outside.)*

GEORGE: Those kids are really growing, aren't they?

LILLY: Oh, that Chase looks just like Preston for the world. Same eyes. Same smile.

GEORGE: Yeah, and little Chelsea. She's just a sweetheart. Lots of people say she looks like Lilly. I think so too. 'Specially the way she carries herself. Don't you think, Gerald?

JERRY *(changing the subject):* I saw Louise Nash from next door.

LILLY *(a little worried):* Oh? Well, did you wave to her over the fence or something?

JERRY: No, Mom. I had a conversation with her.

GEORGE: That Louise—she's a little crazy, you know.

LILLY: She's a lot crazy. Did she tell you about Herbert running off to Albany?

GEORGE: Guess he'd had all he could take.

JERRY: She told me. She also told me something else. Actually, she didn't really tell me. She almost told me and then got kind of nervous and left in a big hurry.

LILLY: What in the world? Well, you know, Louise . . .

GEORGE: Last week, she thought aliens were landing in her backyard and going through her trash. That Louise . . .

JERRY: What's going on, Dad?

GEORGE: What do you mean?

JERRY: Louise mentioned something about being glad I was home *under the circumstances*—because of your condition. What's going on?

GEORGE: Well, Son . . . I, uh . . .

(Knock on the front door. PRESTON *enters, causing* GEORGE *and* LILLY *to look relieved.)*

PRESTON: Knock, knock.

LILLY: Oh, Preston, we're really glad to see you.

PRESTON: I wanted to bring by these ledgers and let you look at them over the holidays.

JERRY: Hello, big brother.

PRESTON *(surprised, then brotherly sarcasm takes over):* Well, well, Nanook of the North has come home.

JERRY: Good to see you too, Preston.

PRESTON: I thought we were too civilized for you.

LILLY: Now, boys, what we all need is a piece of Mom's pie and some milk to wash it down with. And then we'll sit down and talk awhile. I'll be right back. *(Exits to kitchen)*

GEORGE *(grabbing his sons around the neck, one under each arm, pulling them close):* It's been a long time since I had both of my boys under one roof. Yes sir. It's like old times.

(Blackout)

Scene 3

(Half an hour later. Scene opens with PRESTON *and* JERRY *sitting at the dining room table. Both are sulking, forks in hand, "playing" with their pie. There is a long silence, finally* JERRY *speaks.)*

JERRY: Mom used to fuss at us about picking at our food like this.

PRESTON *(mumbling):* What do you care?

JERRY: Mom used to fuss at you about mumbling at the table.

PRESTON: What do you care! What do *you* care!

JERRY: Hey, don't get all bent out of shape, Preston. I was just trying to make conversation.

PRESTON *(returns to playing with pie, mumbles):* I don't care . . .

JERRY: What's going on with Dad?

PRESTON *(incensed, looking up from the pie):* What's going on with Dad? I'll tell you what's going on with Dad. Five years of stuff has gone on with Dad and Mom. And where have you been? Iceland or somewhere, rubbing noses with Eskimos.

JERRY: It's the Yukon.

PRESTON: Yeah, right. The Yukon. It's not even a state.

JERRY: They don't have states in Canada. They have provinces.

PRESTON: It's not even a province. It's a territory, for heavens sake. It's ice and snow and outposts and French fur traders named Jacque.

JERRY: It's not like that. Look, I know I've been gone for a while.

PRESTON: A long while, Jerry. In the meantime, life has gone on here. Dad's retired. And Mom—Mom's had a bout with pneumonia and was in the hospital last winter. Did you know that? Did you care?

JERRY: I knew it. I sent her some flowers.

PRESTON: Oh, that was thoughtful. She and Dad have owned a flower farm for 30 years, and you send her flowers.

JERRY: Look, Preston, I know that we've had our differences. In fact, we've been different most of our lives. But why are you hostile to me?

PRESTON: I'm not hostile! Although I have good reason to be.

JERRY: Why? Because I chose to move away and do something sort of . . . different, and you chose to stay here and run the family business? I don't think that's fair, Preston.

PRESTON: Let me ask you something. Do you think it's fair for you to tell Mom and Dad that you were going on a backpacking trip to "find yourself"—and never come back?

JERRY: Never? It's only been five years!

PRESTON: Five years. *Five years.* In five years, I have personally taken this . . . this . . . *business,* this failing flower growing business, and turned it into a gold mine.

JERRY: Dad says you're doing a great job.

PRESTON: Yeah . . . 18-hour days, Jerry. Seven days a week. I work and I work. I hardly ever see my kids. Elizabeth and I have very little relationship left.

JERRY: I'm sorry to hear that. Have you considered counseling?

PRESTON: Have you considered your family's feelings? *I* look after Mom and Dad. *I* sit right here every holiday and see Mom looking sad because her whole family isn't here—again!

JERRY: I never knew that. Mom's always written such upbeat letters. She always sounded like everything was great.

PRESTON: Well, it wasn't.

JERRY: What about Camille? She and her family live a few miles away. I'm sure Mom is glad of that.

PRESTON: Camille? Camille has been gestating for the last five years. She's either carrying a child or wearing one. She doesn't have time to breathe much less time for her parents. When she does come over, she and Dad get into some kind of an argument over the environment or politics or food. They argue about food, Jerry. *(Pause. Then almost as an aside.)* Besides, you've always been Mom's favorite.

JERRY: Give me a break, man. You know that's not true.

PRESTON: Not true? Jerry, you ought to hear her brag on her son—the missionary.

JERRY: I'm not a missionary. I'm a teacher.

PRESTON: Here I am. Working hard, raising a family, even a deacon at church.

JERRY: Deacon? Wow!

PRESTON: And she's so proud of you.

JERRY: If it makes you feel any better, I always knew that you were *Dad's* favorite.

PRESTON: How do you figure that?

JERRY: Well, he talked about your being so responsible, clean-cut, well-behaved . . . a good head for business . . . the work ethic, you know. Me, I was kind of wild and crazy and off-the-wall. Dad didn't—still doesn't—know how to relate to me.

PRESTON: You left, Jerry. You left without saying good-bye.

(JERRY *gathers plates.)*

JERRY: I'm sorry . . .

(JERRY *exits to kitchen.)*

(PRESTON *remains seated at the table, drinking his milk, lost in thought. There is a knock at the front door.* PRESTON *crosses to door, opens it.* JAMES, *the farm hand, is there holding a plate of cookies.)*

PRESTON: Oh, James. What are you doing here?

JAMES: Mr. Preston, I just came from the farm and thought I'd bring these cookies that the wife, Wylene, made. She was makin' 'em for our family gatherin' and thought she'd make a extra batch for ya'll.

PRESTON: That was awfully thoughtful of you, James. You didn't have to do that.

JAMES: Oh, I know. Mr. and Mrs. Saunders have been so good to me and Wylene through the years, givin' us canned goods and homebaked food, especially when one of us was ailin'.

PRESTON: That's nice, James. Real nice.

JAMES: When we all heard 'bout Mr. Saunders' bad report, we were all concerned.

PRESTON: Bad report? What bad report, James?

JAMES: The doctor's report. You know, the test results.

PRESTON *(doesn't understand, but pretends to):* Oh, *that* report. Uh, James, when did *you* hear about my dad and a doctor's report?

JAMES: Two, maybe three weeks ago. We all thought Mr. Saunders looked a little bad, but then we don't see him as often as you do. So we weren't sure if he was sick or not. We're prayin' for him. We all are. Well, I best be goin'. I'll see ya Friday at the farm.

PRESTON: Yeah, thanks, James. And tell your wife we appreciate the cookies.

JAMES *(exiting):* I'll do it. Happy Thanksgiving!

(PRESTON *stands, looks at the cookies, looks at the door for a second or two.)*

PRESTON: Jerry!

(Blackout)

Scene 4

(A few minutes later. PRESTON *and* JERRY *are in* JERRY*'s old room.)*

JERRY: Are you sure that's what James said?

PRESTON: Jerry, he used words like "bad report" and "test results."

JERRY: Well, that makes what Louise Nash said make sense.

PRESTON: Mrs. Nash make sense? That's a first.

JERRY: OK, here's Louise and James—both of them seem to know about Dad's health. And they never said a word to you, Preston?

PRESTON: No. Not a word. I see Mom and Dad almost every day. Sit with them at church. Stop by and see them on my way home some evenings. And to think, James, a hired hand, on the farm knows the most intimate details about my own father's health!

JERRY: Do you think Camille knows?

PRESTON: I'm sure she doesn't if we don't. Why do you think they wouldn't tell us that Dad's sick . . . that he may be . . . may be . . .

JERRY: Dying?

PRESTON: We don't know for sure . . . I mean, we just heard that he got some bad lab reports. We don't even know what's wrong. Besides, this is the '90s. There's treatment and surgery . . . maybe he's not going to . . . to . . .

JERRY: Die? It's OK to say it, Preston. Death happens, you know. Even if we don't like to talk about it, it still happens.

PRESTON: It happened to our little brother, Jody, and we never talked about that. *(Lights up downstairs. Blackout in bedroom.* CAMILLE, LILLY, *and* GEORGE *enter from kitchen.)*

LILLY: I thought Jerry might be out back. I'm not sure where he is. I know he can't wait to see you.

CAMILLE: Well, tell him I'll see him tomorrow. I want to hear everything about my little brother.

LILLY: Camille, honey, I think it was a good idea your coming over this evening bringing some of the children's things so you wouldn't have to bring so much tomorrow.

CAMILLE: Well, Mama, the diapers alone take up the whole backseat of the van. Then, of course, we have to bring *our* food.

GEORGE: Camille, your mother's going to have plenty of food.

CAMILLE: Not organically grown food, Daddy. Do you know how many chemical fertilizers they use to grow one spear of asparagus?

LILLY: I'm not serving asparagus.

CAMILLE: I'll bring some from my garden. I canned some last summer.

LILLY: Well, OK. But I've got turkey and dressing—and pumpkin pie.

CAMILLE: Mother! I'm not going to eat that. Those things are full of preservatives.

GEORGE: Young lady, your mother has worked hard preparing a traditional Thanksgiving meal. I should think you'd be grateful!

LILLY: It's all right, George.

GEORGE: Just think of the starving children around the world who'd love to have a meal like your mother's serving tomorrow. And another thing, when I was a boy we never had food like that. No sir. We were lucky if we got meat once a week, and when we did, we had to go out and kill it ourselves!

LILLY: George, don't get upset. Please!

(GEORGE *turns to exit to kitchen.)*

CAMILLE: Mother, maybe we shouldn't even come for Thanksgiving dinner tomorrow!

LILLY: Oh, no, honey. Don't stay away! It's the first holiday in five years we've all been together. *(Begins to cry)* Please don't stay away.

CAMILLE: Oh, Mother, I'm sorry. Don't get so upset. You know how it is with Daddy and me. We hardly ever agree on anything.

LILLY: Just this once, Camille, could you not fight with your father. He's—well, please let's just overlook our differences, huh?

CAMILLE: But, Mother, Daddy's always treating me like a little girl. And he doesn't like Chuck at all. He wanted me to marry a doctor or a lawyer—a boring lawyer!

LILLY: You're his only daughter. No man will ever be good enough for you. You know that. Please, honey, for my sake. Let's have a peaceful holiday, all right?

CAMILLE: OK.

LILLY: Bring your asparagus, if you like. I'll put it in a casserole dish and your father will never know.

CAMILLE *(smiling, shaking her head):* Always the peacemaker.

LILLY: I need to see about your father. Can you let yourself out, honey?

CAMILLE: Sure, Mom. *(Hugs* LILLY *before exiting to kitchen)*

LILLY: See you tomorrow.

(Knock on front door)

CAMILLE *(from kitchen):* I'll get it, Mom.

(Crosses and opens door. ANDY, *the delivery boy, is there.)*

CAMILLE: Hi, can I help you?

ANDY: I'm Andy from Hancock's Drugstore. Is Mr. Saunders in?

CAMILLE: Yes . . . he's not feeling well. I'm his daughter.

ANDY: Not feeling well, huh? Oh, I guess he's needing his medication. I know that Mr. Saunders does start feeling bad when the medication wears off. This should help. *(Hands bag)*

CAMILLE: That's a lot of medicine.

ANDY: Well, it helps with the pain.

CAMILLE: The pain?

ANDY: It's something that people with your father's condition have to deal with. This medicine should help. Would you sign here? *(Hands her the clipboard and a pencil)*

(CAMILLE *looks shocked; mechanically signs the paper.)*

ANDY: Thanks. Happy Thanksgiving! *(Exits)*

(CAMILLE, *still in shock, looks at the medicine, tosses it on the table, and hurriedly exits to outside.)*

(Blackout)

Scene 5

(Later that evening. LILLY *is standing at the table polishing the silver flatware. She counts the spoons—11—counts again—still 11. Sits down at the table and begins to cry.* GEORGE *enters from kitchen.)*

GEORGE: Lil? *(Noticing his wife)* Lilly, what's the matter?

LILLY *(crying):* There's only 11 spoons.

GEORGE: Eleven spoons?

LILLY *(crying):* There's supposed to be 12, but there's only 11.

GEORGE: Don't cry, honey. Maybe you counted wrong.

LILLY: No, I counted twice. There's only 11!

GEORGE: It's probably in the buffet—or maybe it's mixed in with the stainless—or it fell behind something.

LILLY *(interrupting):* You wouldn't kill the dandelions!

GEORGE: The dandelions? Lilly, what are you talking about? What does that have to do with silverware?

LILLY: For years, I tried to get you to do something about the dandelions in the backyard. But you never did.

GEORGE: Is that what this is all about? Dandelions in the backyard?

LILLY: You wouldn't allow one tiny weed to live among the flowers at the farm, but you let them grow everywhere in your own backyard.

GEORGE: I never saw much harm in that.

LILLY: But they're weeds, George.

GEORGE: I know. I tried to control them, but . . . *(Pauses, sees this is getting him nowhere.)* Why didn't you tell me this years ago, Lilly? Have you always felt this way about dandelions in the backyard?

LILLY: Yes. I pretended like it didn't bother me.

GEORGE: You weren't being honest. You know, I wasn't honest either.

LILLY: What?

GEORGE: Well, I never told you, but I didn't try very hard to get rid of the dandelions. Fact is, I've always liked dandelions. They're pretty.

LILLY: They're weeds!

GEORGE: I know that. *(Pauses, trying to think)* Lilly, there's been a lot of pain in our 40-plus years of marriage. Most of the pain we didn't talk about. Problems with money, conflicts with our children, even Jody's death.

LILLY: I don't want to talk about that.

GEORGE: Then don't talk. Listen. There are lots of things I wish had been different. Lots of mistakes. Maybe I should have killed the dandelions, but I don't think we should ever hide the way we feel.

LILLY: George, I don't want to lose you.

GEORGE: Oh, so that's what this is all about. It's not really about weeds or spoons, is it?

LILLY: No.

GEORGE: You know, Lil, this recent thing with my health, the tests and all that, have made me realize how fragile life can be. I don't think we have time to mince words—to leave things unsaid.

LILLY: Oh George . . .

(GEORGE *hugs* LILLY.)

GEORGE: Come on, I'll help you look for that spoon.

(GEORGE *and* LILLY *exit to kitchen.)*

(CAMILLE, *from downstage right, crosses to porch.* PRESTON *and* JERRY *enter through outside door.)*

JERRY: OK, OK. We'll talk to Mom and Dad tomorrow.

PRESTON: I wanted to talk to them now . . . before everybody gets here tomorrow.

JERRY: Everybody? Who else besides Camille and her family are coming?

PRESTON *(disdainfully):* Oh, Aunt Saucy and Uncle Herman.

JERRY: Oh great! I love them.

PRESTON: You can't be serious, Jerry. Aunt Saucy? The woman is a clown.

JERRY: Just a little eccentric.

PRESTON: And Herm the worm? He collects spoons, for heaven's sake.

JERRY: That's what I like about him. He's focused.

PRESTON: Focused—on spoons?

JERRY: He has to focus on something. Aunt Saucy won't let him get a word in edgewise. Does he still work at the ice cream factory?

PRESTON: Oh yes. He's worked his way up to chocolate vat supervisor.

JERRY: Hey, all right, Herm! What a guy!

(Enter CAMILLE *from porch.* JERRY *and* PRESTON *do not see her at first.)*

PRESTON: Jerry, you're such a child.

JERRY: At least I'm not boring.

PRESTON: What do you mean by that?

JERRY: Face it, Preston. You're afraid to color outside the lines—to take a risk at anything—to be different.

PRESTON: Oh yeah? Well, at least I don't . . .

CAMILLE *(interrupting):* Oh, I see sibling rivalry is still alive and well at the Saunders' house.

JERRY: Camille! Where did you come from?

CAMILLE: Hey, little brother. I was out on the porch. It's starting to get a little cool.

(JERRY *and* CAMILLE *embrace.)*

JERRY: Well, you're looking—pregnant! In fact, I think you looked like this when I saw you five years ago.

PRESTON: And every day since.

CAMILLE *(to* JERRY, *sarcastically):* Preston and I still adore each other too.

JERRY: Nothing's changed. Hey, where's Chuck and that army of kids of yours?

CAMILLE: They'll be here tomorrow. I was here earlier and brought some things. And then the strangest thing happened—the drugstore delivered some medicine. I went for a walk.

PRESTON: Camille . . . what do you know?

CAMILLE: I had to think . . .

JERRY: So, you know something's up too?

(Blackout)

ACT II

Scene 1

(Thanksgiving morning. Lights up on stage left bathroom. LILLY *is fixing her hair;* GEORGE *is shaving.)*

GEORGE: Feeling better this morning?

LILLY: Yes, a little. Thank you for helping me find the spoon.

GEORGE: Ah . . .

LILLY: I enjoyed our talk too. I'm glad to know how you feel.

GEORGE: I'd like to know more often how *you* feel.

LILLY: Yes, I guess you would, George. Did you call your sister yesterday?

GEORGE: Yes, I did. Saucy and Herman will be here today just like they said they would.

LILLY: Did you tell them what time to be here?

GEORGE: Eleven o'clock, honey. Just like every Thanksgiving.

LILLY: She's not bringing anything, is she? I mean, you told her not to bring any food, didn't you?

GEORGE: I told her not to—just like every Thanksgiving, but I suspect she'll bring something anyway. She always does.

LILLY: Oh, I hope it's not that oyster pie again. Chase got so sick last year from eating that pie.

GEORGE: I don't think he was sick from eating the pie. I think he got sick when he found out what was *in* the pie. He turned an interesting shade of green, as I remember.

LILLY: Well, I'm not going to subject my family to Aunt Saucy's cooking this year. I'll dump it down the garbage disposal, and then tell her that I dropped it, or something.

GEORGE: Now, Lil. *(Suddenly)* Owwww!

LILLY *(alarmed):* George, what's the matter? Do you need your medicine? Oh, please, Lord, help!

GEORGE: Calm down, Lillian. I just nicked myself shaving, that's all.

LILLY: Oh, George, I'm not handling this very well . . . jumping every time you have a pain.

GEORGE: There's some tough times ahead of us . . . according to the doctors. They don't even know what all's in store for me yet. But, honey, there are people praying for me already, and I've got good doctors. This is kinda like those dandelions in the backyard.

LILLY: Are we gonna talk about that again?

GEORGE: If you like.

LILLY: George, we have to be honest. I haven't always been.

GEORGE: Does that mean you want to tell the children about my illness?

LILLY *(nods her head):* I want to talk to them about lots of things. About how I feel. About the good things and bad things. I don't want to pretend that everything's perfect anymore. I'd like to learn how to start accepting the weeds.

GEORGE: There ya go . . .

(GEORGE *and* LILLY *embrace.)*

(Blackout on upstairs left. Lights up downstairs, PRESTON *enters from outside door.)*

PRESTON *(to offstage):* Chase, you keep an eye out for Chelsea, OK? Don't leave the yard.

(ELIZABETH *enters carrying casserole dish.)*

PRESTON: Elizabeth, Mom said not to bring food.

ELIZABETH: She says that every year, Preston. But every year *everybody* brings something. Your Aunt Saucy will bring some awful, outrageous concoction. Your sister Camille will bring some natural thing—wild honey and tree bark or something. And I will have something too. Beatrice's sweet potato soufflé!

PRESTON: Mom's not gonna be happy.

ELIZABETH: Your mom's never happy with me anyway.

PRESTON: That's not true.

ELIZABETH: I'm not stupid, Preston. I know your mother doesn't like me. She thinks I'm—uppity or something.

PRESTON *(mumbling, sarcastically):* Can't imagine why she'd think that.

ELIZABETH: What did you say?

PRESTON *(trying to recover):* Oh, I said. I can't imagine what to drink with that . . . that . . . soufflé. Iced tea, maybe.

ELIZABETH: Uh-huh. I'm gonna put this out in the kitchen.

(ELIZABETH *exits to kitchen.)*

PRESTON: Mom and Dad should be down in a little while. I'm going to sit out on the porch and read the paper.

(PRESTON *crosses to porch; sits on bench; begins to read the newspaper.)*

(JERRY *enters downstage right; crosses to porch.)*

JERRY: Brother . . .

PRESTON: Brother . . .

JERRY: It's nice out here today.

PRESTON: Uh huh.

JERRY: So . . . what are we gonna do?

PRESTON: You mean about talking to Dad?

JERRY: Here's what I think. I think you should ask him what's going on.

PRESTON: Me? Why me?

JERRY: You're the oldest. He likes you. Besides, you and Dad are close.

PRESTON: Oh yeah. We're real close, Jerry. One of his employees knows more about him than I do.

JERRY: I think they're just trying to protect us. Mom's always liked to deal with things by saying, "Let's don't talk about it."

(CAMILLE *enters downstage right, crossing to porch.)*

CAMILLE *(overhearing):* That was her response to everything.

JERRY: Hi, sis. Where's the family?

CAMILLE: They're coming later. I thought we three could talk some more, and maybe we could decide how to talk to Mom and Dad.

PRESTON: We can talk all we want, but if they won't talk back, we won't know any more than we did before.

CAMILLE: Mom's always avoided conflict. She never talked about anger, or sadness—or sex, for that matter.

PRESTON: Camille!

CAMILLE: Well, it's true. We never talked about sex.

PRESTON: Trash mouth.

JERRY: Come on, Preston. Enough's enough. We're grown-ups now.

PRESTON *(mumbling):* Some of us are . . .

CAMILLE: Cheap shot!

PRESTON: Baby factory!

CAMILLE: Take it back.

PRESTON: Will not!

CAMILLE: You're not the boss of me . . .

JERRY: Please! Would you listen to yourselves? You act like we're kids again.

CAMILLE: I wish we were . . .

JERRY: Why?

CAMILLE: 'Cause things were a lot simpler when we were kids. No responsibilities, no problems . . .

PRESTON: There were problems! Plenty of problems.

JERRY: We never talked about 'em.

PRESTON: No, we didn't. I knew things weren't perfect, but I never said anything. I never told anybody how I felt . . . when I was sad.

CAMILLE: You mean . . . like when Jody died?

JERRY: That's the first time I've ever heard you mention Jody, Camille.

CAMILLE: I assumed you didn't feel the same way I did. I remember getting all dressed up for the funeral. We came home and nobody said anything. You boys didn't seem to miss him like I did.

JERRY: I missed him a lot. We never even talked about the accident.

PRESTON: It was too painful.

CAMILLE: I needed someone. Mom was trying to be strong for everybody. Daddy and I never could communicate.

JERRY: And we three were so different, we didn't have much in common.

PRESTON: Nothing's changed in that area.

JERRY: It needs to change. It *can* change. We can't let this happen again. Here's another crisis, maybe with Dad. We can't pretend it doesn't exist this time.

CAMILLE: I love Mom and Dad.

PRESTON: So do I.

JERRY: That's one thing we have in common. And if Dad's sick and he needs us, we ought to be able to be honest with our parents even if they're afraid of being honest with us.

PRESTON: Honesty, there's a novel idea. Elizabeth and I could use a good dose of it.

CAMILLE: We all could, Preston.

(Blackout)

Scene 2

(A few minutes later. Enter SAUCY *and* HERMAN *from outside door.* HERMAN *carries a covered dish.)*

SAUCY *(with flourish):* Happy Turkey Day, everybody!

LILLY *(entering from kitchen):* Saucy, Herman. Come in.

(Enter ELIZABETH *from kitchen.)*

SAUCY: Lillian, my favorite sister-in-law! Happy Thanksgiving! And, Liz, how are you?

ELIZABETH *(correcting):* It's Elizabeth . . .

SAUCY: Of course. But we're all family. We can have pet names for each other, can't we? Do you know how I got the name "Saucy"?

ELIZABETH: As a matter of fact . . .

SAUCY: My big brother, Georgie, gave it to me. When he was little, he couldn't pronounce my real name . . . Prudence. That's my given name. Tried to say "sister" and it came out "Saucy." Isn't that cute?

ELIZABETH *(sarcastically):* Darling.

GEORGE *(entering from kitchen):* Hey, Baby Sister.

SAUCY: There's my Georgie! Come here and hug your little Saucy Mae!

(SAUCY *hugs* GEORGE *aggressively.)*

GEORGE: And, Herman. How are you?

SAUCY: Don't just stand there, Herman. Say something.

HERMAN: We brought you a pie. *(Hands her the pie)*

LILLY: Oh, you shouldn't have, really . . .

HERMAN: It's got oysters in it.

GEORGE: Oh . . .

SAUCY: I saw the look on Chase's face last year when he ate some of my oyster pie, and I says to myself, "As long as Saucy Brown draws breath, she'll bring that boy an oyster pie every Thanksgiving." That's what I said. Standing right over there, I think it was.

GEORGE: Well, why don't you both sit down. Saucy . . . Herman. Take a load off. (SAUCY *and* HERMAN *cross to couch and sit.* GEORGE *crosses behind them.* LILLY *crosses to the table.)*

LILLY: I'll put the pie over here in a safe place. George, have you seen Jerry yet this morning?

SAUCY: Jerry? Little Jerry's home? You don't mean it! Why, where is my little dumplin'? I can't wait to give him a big ol' sloppy kiss.

(JERRY, PRESTON, *and* CAMILLE *enter from porch.)*

JERRY: Did I hear my name in vain?

SAUCY: Oh, sugarplum. My Jerry has come home. *(Hugs* JERRY *aggressively)*

LILLY: Preston, Camille. I didn't know you were here.

CAMILLE: We haven't been here long.

PRESTON: We wanted to talk . . .

JERRY: Aunt Saucy, it's good to see you. Uncle Herman.

SAUCY: Say something, Herman.

HERMAN: We brought a pie.

GEORGE *(to* CAMILLE): What were you talking about?

CAMILLE: Things, Daddy.

GEORGE: What kinds of things?

CAMILLE: Just different things.

LILLY: So, Herman, how's the ice cream business?

HERMAN: It's very rewarding.

JERRY: Preston tells me you got a promotion.

SAUCY: Oh, I signed Herman up for a Dale Carnegie course. You know, that "How to Win Friends and Influence People" thing. And it's made all the difference in Herman's personality. Tell 'em about it.

HERMAN: Well . . .

SAUCY *(interrupting):* I mean, he got promoted to vat supervisor the very next day after he graduated from the study course. Tell 'em, Herman.

HERMAN: Well . . .

SAUCY *(interrupting):* Herman really came out of his shell . . .

JERRY: How's your spoon collection, Uncle Herman?

(Lines nearly on top of each other with HERMAN*'s remarks being basically ignored.)*

HERMAN: Oh, I have some very interesting specimens . . .

SAUCY: Oh, yes. His brother, Harvey, sent him a spoon all the way from Ottawa. That's in Canada.

LILLY: You know, Jerry lives in Canada. In the Yukon . . .

PRESTON: It's not a state. Not even a province . . .

HERMAN: My spoon from Ottawa has a horse on the handle.

ELIZABETH: Really?

PRESTON: No, it's a territory.

HERMAN: I went to Ottawa once . . .

SAUCY: It's very cold in Canada. I'll bet you know that, don't you, Jerry?

GEORGE: He's a teacher.

LILLY: He's a missionary.

HERMAN: While I was in Ottawa, I saw lots of interesting things . . .

CAMILLE: Yukon's not a province? I didn't know that . . .

HERMAN: But I don't remember seeing any horses up there . . .

ELIZABETH: If it's not a province, what is it?

PRESTON: It's a territory.

SAUCY: You're a missionary, Jerry? Oh, Aunt Saucy's so proud of you, darling.

HERMAN: But my spoon has a horse on it. I didn't see any horses when I was up there.

GEORGE: Of course, Preston's a deacon in our church. That's mission work, too, you know.

PRESTON: Dad, you don't have to defend me.

JERRY: I'm not really a missionary.

CAMILLE: You're not?

(Suddenly!)

HERMAN *(standing and shouting):* There are no horses in Ottawa!

(Everyone freezes, shocked. HERMAN *looks at the others, then begins to sit slowly as he speaks.)*

HERMAN: I never . . . saw . . . any . . . horses . . . in Ottawa.

(Enter CHELSEA *and* CHASE *from outside. Everyone looks uncomfortably at each other.)*

CHELSEA: When are we gonna eat, Grandma?

CHASE: Yeah, I'm starving.

LILLY: Oh, well . . . soon. Your Uncle Chuck and your cousins haven't gotten here yet.

CAMILLE: Yeah, I wonder where they are. Maybe I'll call Chuck and see what's keeping them. *(Exits to kitchen)*

LILLY: I need to check on the turkey. *(Exits to kitchen)*

ELIZABETH: I'll warm up the soufflé. *(Exits to kitchen)*

SAUCY: I'll go ahead and slice the pie I brought. *(Exits to kitchen)*

CHASE: Pie?

(PRESTON *clamps his hand over* CHASE's *mouth.)*

(Blackout)

Scene 3

(Ten minutes later. GEORGE *and* LILLY *stand at center as* GEORGE *convenes the family.)*

GEORGE: All right, everybody. The cook tells me it's time to eat. So, let's gather round.

LILLY: As always, the food's there in the kitchen. You'll fix your plate. Kids, there's a table set up for you in the kitchen. Grown-ups, you can sit out here in the dining room.

(SAUCY, ELIZABETH, *and* CAMILLE *enter from kitchen.* HERMAN, PRESTON, JERRY, CHASE, *and* CHELSEA *cross to center.)*

CHELSEA: Where's Uncle Chuck?

GEORGE: Aunt Camille says that he and the kids will be here later. Taylor was napping, Katie needed a nap.

CAMILLE *(lightheartedly interrupting):* The truth is, Uncle Chuck's watching the football game. They'll be here in time for dessert probably.

GEORGE: As you know, there's a Saunders tradition at Thanksgiving. In this basket are some kernels of corn. Each person takes a kernel and then tells of one thing that he or she is thankful to God for.

CHELSEA: Can I go first?

LILLY: Sure, honey. I think it's only fair that the youngest one starts.

CHELSEA *(takes a kernel):* I'm thankful for my family.

CHASE *(whining):* Ah, that's what I was gonna say. Mom, she took mine.

ELIZABETH: Think of another one, Chase.

CHASE: Ah, I can't.

PRESTON: What about being thankful for our country?

CHASE *(reluctantly, takes a kernel):* OK. I'm thankful for our country.

HERMAN: That's what I was gonna say.

SAUCY: Herman!

HERMAN *(pouting, takes a kernel):* I'm thankful for my job.

SAUCY *(takes a kernel):* I'm thankful to God for my health.

ELIZABETH *(takes a kernel):* I'm thankful for prosperity.

CAMILLE *(takes a kernel):* I'm thankful for new life!

JERRY *(takes a kernel):* I'm thankful to God for freedom.

PRESTON *(takes a kernel):* I'm thankful for security!

LILLY *(takes a kernel):* I'm thankful for—honesty.

(JERRY, PRESTON, *and* CAMILLE *look puzzled at each other.)*

CAMILLE: Did you hear what you just said, Mom?

LILLY: Yes, honey. I did. I'm thankful that we can be honest with the ones we love.

(Pause)

JERRY: Why don't we start with what's going on now, Mom? We all suspect something's not right with Dad.

GEORGE: Well, OK. *(Looking at* LILLY) Lil?

LILLY: Go ahead, George.

GEORGE: I went to the doctor a few weeks ago. I got kind of a bad report. It's cancer.

(All look sadly at each other.)

CAMILLE: So, we were right.

PRESTON: Why didn't you tell us?

LILLY: I wouldn't let him. I keep thinking that if we don't talk about it, it'll go away.

GEORGE: The doctors have started me on some medication. Then, there may be surgery—maybe other treatments—we don't know now.

ELIZABETH: Is there anything we can do?

GEORGE: Sure, lots of things. Pray for me. Talk to me. Listen to me.

CHELSEA: Grandpa, are you gonna die?

GEORGE: Oh, everybody's gonna die, Chelsea. But right now I'm living—and I want to enjoy it.

JERRY: I've got something else to be thankful for. Is that allowed?

GEORGE: Sure.

JERRY: I'm thankful for differences. We're all unique, and I'm thankful for that.

CAMILLE: Me too. And I'm thankful for love and acceptance in spite of our differences.

PRESTON: I'm thankful for hard times.

(ELIZABETH *looks puzzled at* PRESTON. PRESTON *reaches out and takes* ELIZABETH'S *hand.)*

PRESTON: The hard times don't have to break us. They can make us stronger. In fact, I'm praying they will. *(Pause)* Your turn, Dad.

GEORGE *(takes a kernel):* Well, I . . . I am thankful . . . for . . . dandelions.

PRESTON: Dandelions?

CAMILLE: What do you mean, Daddy?

JERRY: Yeah, explain.

GEORGE: Well . . . now I didn't ask you to explain your answers.

CHASE: Yeah, but our answers weren't weird like yours, Grandpa.

ELIZABETH: Chase!

GEORGE: That's OK, Elizabeth. Maybe Chase is right. Maybe what I said was a little weird. Chase, your grandmother reminded me that we had dandelions in the backyard. Of course, I knew that, but it started me thinking. You know, dandelions are awfully stubborn . . . strong roots. And the little flower that pops up . . . it's kinda fragile. I mean, a puff o' wind comes along and the petals blow away and . . .

JERRY *(interrupting):* What are you trying to say, Dad?

GEORGE: Well, Son. What I'm trying to say is, I think we're like a yard full of dandelions. Our family. What's on the surface here is kinda fragile, but even though we may have to dig down a little to find 'em, we've got strong roots. OK, so I didn't control the weeds. I let 'em grow wild in my own backyard. But I don't regret it—no sir. I don't regret a few harmless . . . beautiful . . . weeds.

(Thoughtful pause)

HERMAN: One man's aggravation is another man's garden.

(Astonished pause)

JERRY: Uncle Herman, that's a beautiful thought. Did you read that in a book somewhere?

HERMAN: No, I just now made it up.

SAUCY: Herman? You made that up? Oh, I knew that Dale Carnegie course would do you some good.

(All begin to exit to kitchen.)

(Blackout)

Scenes from Love's Café

Characters

STORYTELLER: an older female, Christine "aged" (may be an offstage voice)

HENRY LOVE: a kind Christian man

MAVIS LOVE: his gentle Christian wife

CHRISTINE: waitress, through whose eyes this story is seen

STRANGER: a traveling businessman

PEARL BARKER: Mavis Love's mother

GENEVA TUCKER: a Yankee who moves to town

WAYLON: a Barney Fife type lawman

SAMMY DALE DRAPER: a salesman

REVELINE MYERS: county health nurse

WENDELL, JR.: as a 10-year-old

WENDELL, JR.: as an adult

MATTIE: Mavis's sophisticated sister

JAMES: Mattie's grown son

SANDRA: James's wife

CAFÉ CUSTOMERS and PARADE PARTICIPANTS

Approximate Playing Time: 75 minutes

Setting

The deep South. A small café in the town of Pondtown. An entrance door from the outside at upstage right. Two or three café tables and chairs at center stage. Upstage center a counter with bar stools. Upstage left may have a booth (optional).

Time Changes

All the action takes place in the café over a 50-year period. Characters "age" during scene changes. This can be achieved easily with costume changes that reflected the decade and with graying hair spray and/or wigs, and with makeup. Actors can learn to do this quick aging trick: Dab foundation on wrinkle points while tightening the face (squinting eyes, drawing corners of mouth, bowing lips). When the face relaxes, the foundation leaves natural wrinkles that the characters would then fill in with light gray or red eye pencil. They should then powder face gently to set the foundation and to give the face a matte look. Some of the characters may add pounds with "belly" padding. Aging will be accentuated with a little stooping of the shoulders and a slower walk. The younger and the older Wendell, Jr., might be played by son and father who look alike.

Props

Food items
Menus
Pads
Pencils
Baby carriage or pram *(appropriate for 1940s)*
Brochure
Christmas decorations
Fourth of July decorations
Decorations for wedding reception

Costumes

Costumes change with each scene appropriate to the decade. "Lady Liberty" (PEARL BARKER, Scene II) should be dressed in a toga and a Statue of Liberty headpiece. She carries a torch. All looking quite homemade. REVELINE wears a nurse's uniform, preferably the gray version. WAYLON wears a law enforcement uniform. All others dress according to their characters.

Scene 1

TIME: Summer 1942

(As scene opens we hear 1940s Big Band music as if coming from a juke box. STORYTELLER *stands to one side of the stage.)*

STORYTELLER: It was June 8, 1942. I remember it 'cause it was the same day little Jimmy Barker jumped out of the window over at the schoolhouse. It was in the paper—the *Pondtown Gazette.* Still got the clipping in my scrapbook. *(Music fades)* Seems it was the last day of school and Jimmy, well, he always was a real rounder, ya know. Jimmy, he took a dare and just kinda sailed out an open window. Everybody thought he was dead at first, but he wasn't. Just had the concussion real bad. Doc said he'd be just fine one day—but he wasn't. Never was right after that. Kinda looked funny out of his eyes.

(Enter HENRY *and* MAVIS *from kitchen. They begin to set tables and get the place ready for business.)*

Anyhow, I remember that day. Same day Love's Café opened for business. Henry and Mavis Love had bought the old mining office building down on Main and set it up real nice. Had tablecloths an' ever'thing. See, it was during the war, but Henry he didn't have to go. Something 'bout a noise in his heart that was caused by the fever when he was a boy. Rheumatic fever, I think it was. Anyhow . . . Henry and Mavis, they sold her daddy's farm after he passed on, and so they took part a the money and opened the café.

Now Mavis, she knew 'bout cookin'. Her being the oldest girl on the farm, why, she learned as a little bitty thing how to cook for the hired hands. Yeah, you couldn't beat her cornbread and black-eyed peas. People used to come to her mama's house from as far away as Jasper to watch Mavis cook cornbread, but so far as I know, nobody ever could fix it as good as Mavis . . . not even her mama.

Anyhow, Henry took her as his bride. Mavis, that is. He took Mavis. They lived with her mama and daddy for a while, and then her daddy took sick and passed on. Then Mavis's oldest brother, Sam, he was sent overseas and got killed by the Germans. Her sister, Mattie, grew up and married away. Her littlest brother . . . well, I already told what happened to little Jimmy . . . and her mama, well she wasn't able to keep up the farm. So, Henry and Mavis sold the old homeplace, sent half the money to her sister Mattie in Chicago. Then they moved to town with Mavis's mama and little Jimmy—and that's how Love's Café got started.

(Light down on STORYTELLER*, up onstage.)*

HENRY: Well . . . Mavis, what do you think? Think we're ready to open the doors?

MAVIS: I guess I'm as ready as I'll ever be. *(Pause)* Henry, do you think we did the right thing—I mean, taking our part a the money from the farm and riskin' it like this?

HENRY: Now, Mavis, we've been all through this. Daddy Barker was a fine man . . . a good, hardworkin' man. But you know that after he took sick he just let the farm go. Why, the back 40 was nothing but a brush heap, and he had to sell off most of his stock just to pay the mortgage. We couldn't have gotten that farm back in shape . . . not just me and you. And you know your mama and Jimmy's not able . . .

MAVIS: I know . . . I know . . . I just don't wanna get us into somethin' that'll drain us dry, that's all. There's a war on, you know.

HENRY *(taking her hand):* Mavis, we prayed about this—me and you—and we talked to the preacher about it. Then you said that you felt God's smile right there in your heart. Why are you doubtin' now?

MAVIS: I don't know.

HENRY: Didn't we ask the Lord to bless this place?

MAVIS: Yeah.

HENRY: And don't you think He'll be faithful?

MAVIS: Yeah.

HENRY: And didn't we ask Him to let us use this place for His glory?

MAVIS: Yeah.

HENRY: And don't you cook the best cornbread this side of the Mississippi?

(MAVIS *smiles.)*

HENRY: People gotta eat. Besides, this is the '40s . . . times are changin'. Pondtown's changin'. People aren't farmin' as much. Factories are openin' and people don't want to cook at home like they used to. They're workin' downtown and want to stop to eat a good, quick meal. *(Pause)* It'll be all right, Mavis. I know it will. If we lift Him up, the Lord's not gonna let us down.

(Lights dim; HENRY *and* MAVIS *exit to kitchen arm in arm.* CUSTOMERS *enter at front door and take their places at the counter and tables. Characters onstage freeze and stage lights dim a bit. Light up on* STORYTELLER.)

STORYTELLER: And the Lord didn't either—let 'em down, I mean. Why, after 'bout the first week, the place was really jumpin'. See everybody knew 'bout Mavis's cookin' and all, and boy, they couldn't wait to partake. *(Enter* CHRISTINE *from kitchen.)* That's where I come in. See, after word got around 'bout the café, why, Henry knew he needed some help. He couldn't run the cash register and wait tables too. And Mavis, she was busy as a bee in the kitchen. So that's when they hired me. *(Enter* STRANGER *at front door.)* See, my Wendell was sent overseas, and I didn't have nothin' to do; needed the money too. Wendell, he'd send me some of his paycheck, but I couldn't really count on when it'd come, him being so far away and all. So, I started workin' for Henry and Mavis, waitin' tables. Made two dollars a day and all I could eat—plus tips, a course. Money helped out a right smart, too, with the new baby . . . little Wendell, Jr., and all. And I enjoyed talkin' to folks . . .

CHRISTINE *(to* STRANGER): What'll ya have?

STRANGER *(looking at menu):* I'll have the blue plate special, please, ma'am. And don't forget the cornbread.

CHRISTINE: Comin' right up.

STRANGER: Heard 'bout that cornbread. Got quite a reputation—all the way to Tupelo.

CHRISTINE: I'll tell Mavis. She'll be tickled. So, you're from Tupelo, are you? What brings you to Pondtown?

STRANGER: The Greyhound bus! *(Pause to let it sink in)* Get it . . . the Greyhound bus?

CHRISTINE: Got it. Are you on business, or you got kin here?

STRANGER: Actually, sorta both. My Uncle Joshua died last week. I'm his only family . . . and so I'm here to settle his business.

CHRISTINE: Oh yeah. Josh Bean. Sorry to hear 'bout Mr. Bean dyin'.

STRANGER: Well, actually I didn't know my uncle very well. He was sort of . . . different.

CHRISTINE: Yeah, now that you mention it, he was a little curious at that.

STRANGER: Eccentric, I guess would be the polite way to say it.

CHRISTINE: Yeah . . . well, I'll bring that order right up for ya. *(Exits to kitchen)*

(Enter CUSTOMERS *at front door. Characters onstage freeze and stage lights dim a bit. Light up on* STORYTELLER.)

STORYTELLER: Before the café opened, we didn't see very many strangers round Pondtown, but now and again the café seemed to bring in folks that we'd never seen before. It was like Love's was a magnet that drew folks there. Don't know if it was Mavis's cookin' or the Lord bringin' 'em in. See, nobody ever came in through that front door without Henry or Mavis or both tellin' 'em 'bout the Lord. It was like their callin', ya know. Not ever'-body believed, and sometimes those that did took their time 'bout it—but 'cause of Henry and Mavis, the Kingdom, one by one, began to grow—and so did business at Love's Café.

(Enter PEARL *and* MAVIS *from kitchen.)*

MAVIS: OK, now, Mama. Me and Henry are getting so busy these days that we sure do need your help. You don't have to cook or take orders or nothin'. Just greet folks at the door and help 'em find a table.

PEARL: Tell me again what I'm 'sposed say to 'em.

MAVIS: Well, say, "Welcome to Love's Café." Then ask 'em if they want a table or a booth.

PEARL: Then what do I say?

MAVIS: Say, "Well, we have a nice booth or table right over here." Then you lead 'em to their table, give 'em a menu, then tell 'em to enjoy their meal.

(PEARL *mimes rehearsing her part.)*

(Enter HENRY *from kitchen.)*

HENRY: Well, Mother Barker. We sure are glad you're gonna be helpin' us. Sure are.

PEARL: "Welcome to Love's Café. We have a nice booth or table right over here."

HENRY: That's real good, Mother Barker. Real good.

PEARL: I'm nervous, Henry.

MAVIS: You'll do fine, Mama. You'll do just fine. Now let's get you some more menus. I think there's some in the back.

(Enter GENEVA *at front door, pushing stroller. During* STORYTELLER, GENEVA *picks up baby and fusses with him. As lights dim onstage, characters freeze. Light up on* STORYTELLER.)

STORYTELLER: The café got to be the place where young and old alike could come to. It kinda got to be a crossroads, 'specially for folks like Geneva Tucker, Foy Tucker's bride. See, Geneva was a Yankee—from somewheres up north like Wisconsin. Tuck, he met her when he was stationed up there somewhere. Well, right before Tuck got sent overseas, he brought Geneva down to Pondtown to live with his mama, on account of Geneva was in the family way and she didn't have no kin up there.

Tuck's twins was born on May 1. Tuck was killed in France on May 2 . Never even knew 'bout his boys.

We were all tore up 'bout Tuck. But Geneva, she never shed a tear, not even at the funeral. It was like she set her jaw and wouldn't let go. We all figured that's the way Yankees are, so we mostly just let her be. Ever'body 'cept Mavis and Henry 'course. They extended the hand a hospitality even when it wasn't graciously received. They showed the love of God right on, too, even when it seemed like it wasn't doin' no good.

(Light off on STORYTELLER, *up onstage.* HENRY *crosses to* GENEVA.)

HENRY: So, Mizz Geneva. If there's anything that Mavis and me can do for ya . . .

GENEVA: There's nothing you can do, Mr. Love.

HENRY: Well, we know that you don't have no kin down here, 'cept Tuck's mama, and we understand that you two . . .

GENEVA *(interrupts):* You understand correctly, Mr. Love. Missus Tucker and I don't get on very well. She made it real clear from the beginning that I was not good enough for Tuck. I'm a Yankee, you see.

HENRY: Well, I don't think Mizz Tucker means nothin' by that. She's just grievin' over Tuck, that's all.

GENEVA: No, Mr. Love. Tuck's mother hated me from the moment she laid eyes on me. Tuck's death had nothin' to do with it.

HENRY: Well, I jest wanted you to know that Mavis and me, we're prayin' for you and the boys, and Mizz Tucker.

GENEVA: I've never been very—religious . . .

HENRY: Well, we're here if you need us.

GENEVA *(mumbles):* Thank you . . .

HENRY: Mizz Geneva, ya know, "The sun's always shinin' . . . but sometimes we just can't always see it . . ."

(Characters onstage freeze and stage lights dim a bit. Light up on STORYTELLER.*)*

STORYTELLER: Henry always had his little sayin's . . . kinda like a proverb or somethin'. At first, I thought they were just small talk or somethin' he'd read in *Reader's Digest.* But then, I began to figure that they were more like a gift, a gift the Lord gave Henry that made him know exactly what to say to folks. Mavis, she had her gift, too, I mean besides her cornbread cookin'. Hers was a tireless heart a kindness. Henry always said that Mavis was puttin' feet to her faith.

(Fifties music takes us out of scene and continues through blackout and into next scene.)

(Blackout)

Scene 2

Time: July 4, 1956

(Fifties music fades as lights come up on scene. CUSTOMERS *enter from outside, then freeze as light comes up on* STORYTELLER.*)*

STORYTELLER: It was hot the summer of '56. We hadn't had a drop a rain for weeks an' ever'thing was dry as a bone. The farmers had long since given up on their crops. The sweet corn was pure burnt up in the field.

That was the summer after the polio hit Pondtown. Yeah, the polio, it'd left its mark on all of us. Took three of us that year—Reb Davis's baby girl, Little Jimmy Barker, and . . . my husband, Wendell. Strange, Wendell, he'd made it through two wars without so much as a scratch. Then in '55 he took the fever and in a few days he was gone.

It was just me and Wendell, Jr., then. Mavis and Henry were grievin' over Little Jimmy dyin', but they raised my salary to three dollars a day just 'cause they knew I needed it.

(Enter CHRISTINE *and* WAYLON *from kitchen.)*

Anyhow, that summer . . . '56 . . . why, posters around town announced that anybody caught with fireworks on the Fourth a July would be fined a thousand dollars, on account of it being so dry and all and they bein' a fire hazard. 'Course there was some who didn't care 'bout startin' fires, like them mean Tucker twins who were always startin' trouble around and about. I seen 'em out behind the old depot, just shootin' them firecrackers and cherry bombs, throwin' 'em at each other. I called the law to 'em. 'Course by the time the law got there what with parade traffic and all, the boys had already run off.

(Light down on STORYTELLER, *up onstage.)*

WAYLON: Now, Christine, you know I can't do nothin' 'bout them boys 'ess I ketch 'em in the act.

CHRISTINE: So, the word of a law-abidin' citizen ain't good enough no more, huh?

WAYLON: I didn't say that, Christine. It's just that Geneva's always coverin' up for them boys. The more she takes up for 'em, the meaner they get.

CHRISTINE: And the meaner she gets.

WAYLON: Now, Christine, how would you act if you was a Yankee, living down here with no husband, two rowdy yungin's and a mother-in-law who all but tossed you out on the street.

CHRISTINE: That was mean of old Mizz Tucker. Treatin' her own kin like that. I'm not sure what Geneva and the boys would've done if Henry and Mavis hadn't taken her in and helped her get a job at the Cut N' Curl.

WAYLON: Then, they helped her get a scholarship to go to beauty school too.

CHRISTINE: That Henry and Mavis—I swear they both got hearts a gold. I wouldn't a done so much for Geneva . . . she's so mean-spirited. Why, if she weren't the best beautician in town, she'd a lost most of her customers. Not friendly and talkative like Lola . . .

WAYLON: Lola's a gossip.

CHRISTINE: She's *talkative,* Waylon . . .

WAYLON: Yeah, talkative is right. Near 'bout ruined my wife's hair. She'd talk and cut and talk and cut. Before long Betty Jo looked like a boy.

CHRISTINE *(laughing):* I remember that. I thought Betty Jo looked more like a kitchen match—them long, skinny legs and that bright red hair.

WAYLON *(laughing):* She did at that. But anyway, now Geneva's got her a rich, old husband and she won't be workin' at the Cut N' Curl no more.

CHRISTINE: Guess Lola'll get all of Geneva's customers—ever' woman in town will look like a kitchen match.

WAYLON: Well, maybe things'll be better for Geneva now. Who knows? Maybe Althus can do somethin' 'bout them boys a hers . . .

CHRISTINE: I wouldn't count on it. Old Althus don't know he's in the world most of the time. I swear, richest ol' man in town and he's an idiot.

WAYLON: Yeah, he's made a killin' sellin' Cadillacs . . . but he can't find his way to his own showroom half the time.

CHRISTINE: We all know Geneva married him for money—and I reckon he married her 'cause he didn't feel like he'd been punished enough in this life.

WAYLON: Christine!

CHRISTINE: Well, that Geneva's mean as a snake.

(Enter HENRY *and* MAVIS *from kitchen.)*

HENRY: Well, howdy, Waylon. How's the law business?

WAYLON: Howdy, Henry—Mavis.

MAVIS: Waylon, you want a glass o' ice cold lemonade to cool ya off? Got a custard pie coolin' in the window. If you don't think it'll spoil your appetite for Henry's barbecue, I'll cut you a little piece.

WAYLON: Awfully temptin', Mavis.

HENRY *(laughing):* Told Mavis weren't no use to set pies in the window to cool. They'd probably cook on the sill today.

WAYLON: Well, it is awful hot. I'll take you up on that lemonade, Mavis. But I don't wanna ruin my supper—so I'll just have to wait on the pie.

MAVIS: OK. Christine, honey, would you get Waylon some lemonade? *(Exits into kitchen)*

(Enter REVELINE *at front door, sits at table.)*

CHRISTINE *(mumbling as she exits into kitchen):* Might as well . . . there won't be no justice done today.

WAYLON: Hey, now, Henry, when will that barbecue be ready?

HENRY: Oh, 'bout sundown, I reckon.

WAYLON: So, you're gonna torture the whole town for *(looks at watch)* five more hours, huh?

HENRY: Torture?

WAYLON: Yeah, making us set here and smell that barbecue a-cookin'.

HENRY: Well, some things gotta simmer awhile before they're good and ready.

WAYLON: Wouldn't be 4th a July without your barbecue, Henry. Why, you know my mouth starts watering ever' year round Valentine's Day.

HENRY: It'll be ready directly.

(Enter CHRISTINE *with lemonade.)*

HENRY *(to* WAYLON*)*: Enjoy . . .

(Enter GENEVA *and* SAMMY *at front door.)*

GENEVA: Sammy Dale Draper. You oughta be ashamed talking about the red menace right here on Independence Day. Besides you wouldn't know a Communist if you stepped on one.

SAMMY: Exactly my point, Geneva. With a bomb shelter, you'd be prepared for anything from a nuclear explosion to a sneak attack. And you never know 'bout those things.

GENEVA: I'm not buying it, Sammy Dale. No country bumpkin salesman is going to . . .

SAMMY: Just look at this brochure on it, Geneva. Lookee there. This one's got a iron door that's five feet thick. Couldn't nothin' get in there.

GENEVA: Or get out. I've been cooped up in this hole in the ground for 10 years now. If the end of life as we know it is threatened, I wouldn't be any worse off if I went out with it.

SAMMY: But, think of the safety of those fine boys of yours.

GENEVA: You leave my boys out of this . . .

SAMMY: And what 'bout that new husband. Wouldn't want this one to get fried by the enemy, too, now would ya?

GENEVA: Why, Sammy Dale Draper. What an awful thing to say.

(Characters onstage freeze and stage lights dim a bit. Light up on STORYTELLER.*)*

STORYTELLER: It was an awful thing for Sammy Dale to say, but no worse than some of the things that Geneva had said to folks over the past 10 years. Spittin' and spewin'. Ever'body had tried to be nice to Geneva and her boys, but seems with ever' passin' year since Tuck died, Geneva got more and more bitter like. Wouldn't be friendly to nobody—not even hardly to

Henry and Mavis, even after they'd helped her so much. Folks thought her marrying Althus Reeves might hep; that maybe she'd have somebody to talk out her feelin's to. Shoot, old Althus was so deaf, he couldn't hear it thunder, so 'stead of Geneva getting sweeter, she got meaner . . . only then she was mean—and rich.

(Lights off STORYTELLER; *up onstage.)*

GENEVA: Hey! Christine! Where's the water I asked for 10 minutes ago? I mean, it's not like you had to go out and kill it or anything. Land sakes, a body could perish in this heat!

(From another table)

REVELINE *(holding up a glass of water):* Bacteria thrives in this kinda temperature, you know. No tellin' what's lurkin' in this little glass of water.

SAMMY *(moving to* REVELINE'S *table):* Why, Reveline Myers. What a sight for sore eyes you are! Haven't seen you in a coon's age.

REVELINE *(still staring into glass of water):* Saw you last week, Sammy Dale, when you tried to sell me a chafing dish out of the trunk of your car. What kinda junk are you selling now?

SAMMY: Reveline, I'm all through with chafin' dishes and pencil sharpeners, and other handy dandy gadgets.

REVELINE: No more Fuller Brushes?

SAMMY: No more brushes. I'm not selling anything. I'm offering smart, intelligent people like you a chance to invest in something that'll save your life one day.

REVELINE *(still looking at glass):* Disgusting.

SAMMY: Reveline, have you ever heard about germ warfare?

(Characters onstage freeze and stage lights dim a bit. Light up on STORYTELLER.)

STORYTELLER: Reveline Myers. Now there was a sight for ya! She was an army nurse during the war and then she come back to Pondtown and started workin' as the county health nurse. One thing you could say 'bout Reveline, she was zealous. Kids in town and some of the hill folks'd avoid her like the plague. Yessir, she was bound and determined to stamp out any malady in Pondtown—ever'thing from ringworm to Communism. *(Lights off* STORYTELLER)

(Enter 10-year-old WENDELL, JR., *from outside, breathlessly.)*

WENDELL: Mama! Mama! Guess what just happened.

CHRISTINE: Wendell, what in blazes is wrong?

WENDELL: It's Lady Liberty. She's done fell off the float right in the middle of the Fourth of July parade.

CHRISTINE: What? Lady Liberty!

MAVIS: Wendell, what did you say?

WENDELL: Lady Liberty fell off the float, Mizz Love.

MAVIS: That's my mama. She was gonna be Lady Liberty on the Civitan float.

WENDELL: They're bringing her over here right now.

(Enter PEARL *at front door in her disarrayed Lady Liberty costume, with others.)*

MAVIS: Mama, are you all right?

REVELINE: Mizz Barker. Everybody stand back. Give her some air! Mizz Barker. Mizz Barker. You hear me? Looks like heat stroke. She doesn't look good.

(PEARL *is helped onto a chair.* REVELINE *tries to revive her.)*

PEARL: Mattie, is that you?

MAVIS: No, Mama, Mattie's not here. It's Mavis.

PEARL: Where's Mattie? Where's my baby?

MAVIS: Mama, Mattie's living in Chicago now. You know that.

REVELINE: Mavis, was Mattie 'spose to come home for the 4th or something?

MAVIS: No, Mattie hasn't been home in years, Reveline.

CHRISTINE: Yeah, Mattie's become a uppity Yankee and don't want to have nothin' to do with us.

PEARL: Mattie? Mattie?

(Characters onstage freeze and stage lights dim a bit. Light up on STORYTELLER.)

STORYTELLER: The barbecue went on as planned, but Mizz Barker got worse and worse, it seemed. By the next day, she didn't even know her own name. A week later, Mizz Barker passed away.

Mavis's sister, Mattie, did come home—in her fine car and her fancy clothes and putting on airs. She was actin' like she was real grieved 'bout her mama too. I 'spect it was 'cause Mattie Ruth was feelin' guilty on account a she hadn't been home in years. Thought she was too good for us simple folks. But Mavis . . . in the midst a her grievin' . . . she tried to minister to her sister. Didn't do no good, though. After the funeral, Mattie got back in that new sports car of hers and drove on back to Chicago . . . back to her fancy parties . . . and her uppitiness.

(Sixties music takes us out of scene and continues through blackout and into next scene.)

(Blackout)

Scene 3

Time: Christmas 1966

(Music down and under STORYTELLER, *who is lighted at side of stage.)*

STORYTELLER: It was the biggest thing that ever happened in Pondtown. Well, if you don't count the time Deacon Fletcher lost his eye in a note-burning service over at the Baptist Church. See, the church was finally debt-free and the preacher wanted to have a note-burning ceremony to be symbolic of their payin' off their debt. It was a good idea too. Everybody went over to the church that Sunday afternoon. The preacher had got out his charcoal grill and covered the bottom with pea gravel from the parkin' lot. He lit up the fire and then he started the ceremony with prayer and supplication. Well, 'bout 10 minutes into the ceremony, that pea gravel heated up and started poppin' out a there like buckshot. It was a sight. People taking shelter under pews and some of 'em runnin' for their lives. Mister Fletcher tried to cover the grill with a Communion tray—and did too—saved the stained-glass windows, 'cept he lost his eye in the process.

(Lights up onstage; STRANGER *enters at front door and crosses to table. Sits and begins looking at the menu.)*

Well, anyhow, didn't mean to get off on that. The fall of 1966, the Heil company out of Kansas City announced that they would open up a factory in Pondtown. It was mighty excitin', too, 'cause it was the first real national industry to come to us. The plant was 'sposed to bring new families to town . . . and new opportunities . . .

(STORYTELLER *light off. Enter* CHRISTINE *from kitchen.)*

CHRISTINE: What'll ya have?

STRANGER: I'll have the usual.

CHRISTINE: Pardon me?

STRANGER: I'll have my usual. The blue plate special—and don't forget the cornbread.

CHRISTINE: Do I know you?

STRANGER: Ah, I don't expect you to remember me. It's been a long time since I was here last. Over 20 years, I reckon.

CHRISTINE: Oh? Well, what brings you to Pondtown?

STRANGER: The Greyhound bus. *(Pause for joke to sink in)* Get it? The Greyhound bus?

CHRISTINE: Oh, yeah. Now you look kinda familiar. You had kin here?

STRANGER: That's right. My uncle Joshua Bean died, and I came here to sell his things and what-not.

CHRISTINE: Tupelo!

STRANGER: Very good. I'm from Tupelo.

CHRISTINE: Well, what brings you to these parts . . . no, don't tell me—*the Greyhound bus!*

STRANGER: Actually, I'm here on business . . . and pleasure. I'm a sales representative with the Heil Company . . . the one that's opening a factory here?

CHRISTINE: Oh . . . well, I'll be . . . ! How 'bout that? So you'll be living here when the factory opens?

STRANGER: No, I'm headquartered in the Tupelo office, but I'll be passing through here from time to time.

CHRISTINE: Well, good. We'll look forward to seein' ya. Now, ya said that you were here for business and pleasure.

STRANGER: Oh . . . yeah. I think I'll have two pieces of cornbread, please!

(Exit CHRISTINE *into kitchen. Enter* HENRY *from kitchen, crossing to nearby table, starts wiping it.)*

HENRY: Howdy . . .

STRANGER: Howdy. Mr. Love?

HENRY: Yeah?

STRANGER: Mr. Love, did you know that you're standin' on a pot a gold?

HENRY: What? *(Starts looking around on floor)*

STRANGER: Yeah, with the new plant opening here, this property is very valuable.

HENRY: Is that so?

(Enter GENEVA *from door, crosses to table. Enter* MAVIS *from kitchen, crosses to* GENEVA'S *table.)*

STRANGER: Oh yeah. Fast-food restaurant could come in here and make a killin'—or a motor lodge—or a Green Stamp store. Yeah, that's it! S and H Green Stamps! How much you reckon you'd take for this place?

HENRY: I don't know. Never thought much about it.

STRANGER: What if someone was to offer you something for it? Would you consider it?

HENRY: I don't know. Prob'ly not.

STRANGER: Bet you could triple what you paid for it.

HENRY: Think so?

(Enter WAYLON *and* REVELINE, *cross to table.)*

STRANGER: Yeah, you and the Missus could take off to that Miami Beach, live it up and you could have enough left to leave a nice nest egg to your children.

HENRY: Well, me and Mavis, we don't have children. The Lord never blessed us in that way.

(From another table)

GENEVA: It's not like I'm not used to it. Yeah, burying husbands is getting to be a habit with me.

MAVIS: We sure are sorry 'bout Althus. He was a good man.

GENEVA: Good? Yes, I guess he was as good as Althus could be.

MAVIS: At least he went peaceful.

GENEVA: Yeah . . .

MAVIS: Well, I 'spose your boys will be coming in for the holidays soon.

GENEVA: Uh, no. They're, uh . . . busy for the holidays.

(Enter WENDELL, JR., *at front door, as an adult, wearing "hippie" clothes and with long hair.)*

(From another table)

WAYLON: Now, Reveline, don't get your dander all up 'bout it. So far, it's still a rumor.

REVELINE: You know good and well it's not a rumor, Waylon. Those hippies have come into this town with their filthy clothes and long, greasy hair, and they're gonna start a commune out on Goose Hollow Road.

WAYLON: Just how do you know that, Reveline?

REVELINE: Sammy Dale Draper told me.

WAYLON: How does Sammy Dale know?

REVELINE: He's selling vinyl siding, ya know, and one of them long-haired freaks was talkin' to Sammy Dale 'bout some sidin' for an old shack out there. *(Enter* SAMMY DALE *at front door.)* Ain't that right, Sammy Dale?

SAMMY DALE: What?

WAYLON: I ain't never heard of hippies buyin' vinyl sidin'.

REVELINE: Didn't you tell me that one of them hippies came to you to buy sidin'?

SAMMY DALE: No, Reveline. Not siding. It was *last* week when I was sellin' shock absorbers. They needed 'em pretty bad, too, for that VW bus—the one with all the flowers on it? But, what's so wrong about them movin' here and startin' a commune anyway?

REVELINE: What's wrong? Commune—Communism? Don't you get it? 'Sides, they'll tear apart the morals o' this town, that's what. They'll corrupt our young people, and pretty soon they'll all be chewing on that funny weed.

WAYLON: I think you're upset over nothin', Reveline.

REVELINE: Well, just look over your shoulder, Mr. Lawman. That long-haired thing at the counter is none other than Christine's Little Wendell. Remember him? Once upon a time, that was a clean-cut little boy.

SAMMY DALE: Well, you've got a point. *(Begins to exit to front door)*

GENEVA: I'm not sure why I'm telling you all this, Mavis, but Tim's in Europe finding himself—with my money, of course. Jake's in Savannah, toasting his debutante girlfriend—with my money.

MAVIS: I've got a good idea, Geneva. Why don't you come and spend Christmas Eve at our house?

(GENEVA *begins to exit to front door.)*

STRANGER *(standing to leave):* But there's somethin' peculiar 'bout you, Mr. Love.

HENRY: Why, thank ya, son.

STRANGER: Anybody who would turn down that kind of money I'm offering you is mighty peculiar. *(Exits through front door)*

HENRY: Well . . . *(Begins to exit toward kitchen)*

(Characters onstage freeze and stage lights dim a bit. Light up on STORYTELLER.)

STORYTELLER: Peculiar wasn't a word that was used too much to describe Henry Love—least not in the bad way. Henry was diff'rent, though. Think that's why folks thought so much of him. 'Course there was some who didn't understand his and Mavis's way. Then there was some that ever so slowly *did* come to understand . . .

(Carolers sing Christmas carol offstage.)

MAVIS *(waving offstage to carolers and singing with them as she wipes tables):* Merry Christmas!

(Enter MATTIE *at front door.)*

MATTIE: Merry Christmas, Mavis.

MAVIS: Oh, Merry Christmas to you— *(Pause)* Mattie? Mattie Ruth?

MATTIE: It's me, Mavis.

MAVIS: Mattie! *(She rushes over and embraces her.)* Where did you come from, sister? How did you get here? How long can you stay? Well, let me look at you!

MATTIE: I came on the afternoon bus. I'm sorry I didn't send word that I was coming. It was at the last minute . . .

MAVIS *(interrupting):* Where's Harold and the children? Didn't they come?

MATTIE: No, Mavis. They didn't come.

MAVIS: Well, why not? Are they comin' later? Oh, Henry'll be so excited.

MATTIE: Harold and I are—divorced. He gets the children for the holidays.

MAVIS: Oh, no, Mattie, honey. I'm so sorry. Why didn't you tell me? I didn't know.

MATTIE: I figured you didn't want to know. I didn't want to embarrass you.

MAVIS: Embarrass me? What a thing to say . . .

MATTIE: I didn't want to ruin your good name or mama's and daddy's either.

MAVIS: Oh, Mattie.

MATTIE: Mavis, when I was here for Mama's funeral I said some real mean things to you.

MAVIS: Now, Mattie Ruth, you don't need to say no more.

MATTIE: No, I do. I made fun of you for bein' content with this place and for your—calling. I remember sayin' that you'd die one day like Daddy and Mama and Jimmy and that you wouldn't have anything to show for your life.

MAVIS: Now, Mattie . . .

MATTIE: I won't tell you, Mavis, that I didn't mean those words. 'Cause at the time, I did mean 'em. But I was just blind then. Living in a big, fancy house in the city, with a rich and handsome husband, and two little children with baby doll eyes.

MAVIS: Well, you had your dreams. I remember you, Mattie, settin' out on the porch and goin' on and on 'bout livin' in the city and doin' things, about makin' somethin' of yourself. I was proud of you, too, when you went off to state college and got your diploma. We were all proud, Mattie.

MATTIE: You had dreams, too, Mavis. You wanted to make a difference somehow too.

MAVIS: Yeah, I guess I did.

MATTIE: 'Course at the time your dreams didn't sound as exciting as mine—but they were noble.

MAVIS: Yeah, we all gotta do it diff'rent ways. I'll never forget the day you and Harold left for Chicago with stars in your eyes. Gonna set the world on fire, you two.

MATTIE: Yeah, now look at me. Not much to show for my dreams.

MAVIS: Well, you've got children that you can pass along your dreams to.

MATTIE: I don't want to pass along my dreams, Mavis. Mine were selfish. Henry used to say that we all store up some kind of treasure . . . whether we want to or not, and then we leave it behind for all who follow us. I think I've been storin' up the wrong kind of treasure. You knew that all along, didn't you, Mavis?

(MAVIS *puts her arm around* MATTIE, *and the two begin to exit toward kitchen as stage lights dim a bit. Light up on* STORYTELLER.)

STORYTELLER: It had taken Mattie Ruth many a year to realize what's real important in life. And her sister, Mavis, bein' godly and wise like she was, knew that God's greatest blessin's sometimes come out of life's greatest sorrows. Though it was hard for Mavis to see Mattie go off like she did . . . she knew that Mattie might have to find out some things the hard way, even if it took a long time. Like Henry used to say . . . some things need to simmer awhile before they're good 'n' ready. And in Pondtown, where things moved kinda slow anyhow . . . that was particular' true. Christmas was special that year. Mattie Ruth was home, at least for a while . . . and her and Mavis seemed closer than ever. After the holidays, Mattie went back to Chicago to her children—to her life, but this time things were diff'rent . . .

(Seventies music begins, continues under STORYTELLER *and through blackout.)*

(Blackout)

Scene 4

Time: Spring 1973

(The café is decorated for a wedding reception. Seventies music under STORYTELLER.)

STORYTELLER: The war was 'sposed to be over, they said, but it wasn't. In '73 we lost two more of our young boys over in Vietnam—during a ceasefire. "A ceasefire." 'Course Mr. Nixon didn't seem to care, on account a he had problems of his own.

Those years were 'specially hard for me. I didn't lose a son to Vietnam but to Canada. Yeah, Wendell, Jr., he didn't believe in the war and, well, him and some other boys ran off to Canada. It was bad enough, that I didn't see my son for years . . . but, some folks called him a Communist and traitor . . . or worse. Sometimes the family couldn't hardly stand it. They didn't have no right to call him names like that. It hurt real bad.

(Lights up onstage)

But 'course Henry and Mavis kept a lot of us goin'. They'd patch up our hearts ever' day or so . . . comfortin' words . . . time off to let some of us cry . . . even wrote encouragin' letters to Wendell too. It got me and the family through.

'Course there always was a lot a love at Love's Café.

(Enter HENRY *from kitchen, trying to tie his bow tie.)*

HENRY: Mavis! Mavis! Can you hep me with this thing. *(Enter* MAVIS *from kitchen.)* Ah, I never could tie one of these here bow ties.

MAVIS: Hold still. Let me do it. Your collar's gonna be black as soot you handlin' it so much. *(Knots the tie)* There. Don't you look spiffy.

HENRY: Look like I just been laid out for my final showin'.

MAVIS: Oh, Henry. You look distinguished. You look like a real father of the bride. Geneva's real proud you agreed to give her away.

HENRY: Well, I'm proud to do it. I'm just glad she met somebody. I think Charlie's a nice man, don't you? Got a good, decent job at the plant. Geneva ain't got much of Althus's money left. So, it must be love.

MAVIS: Don't reckon she got much for the Cadillac dealership, what with the energy crunch on.

HENRY: Folks don't want them gas guzzlers no more.

MAVIS: Ever'body's drivin' them little foreign things. What are they called?

HENRY: Datsuns.

MAVIS: Oh yeah. Datsun—like the weiner dog.

HENRY: No, Mavis. A weiner dog is a dachshund. But come to think of it, them little cars do kinda look like a short-legged dog runnin' down the street. *(They laugh.)*

MAVIS: I know some folks don't like Geneva on account a her being plain-spoken, but she's a good person in a lot a ways.

HENRY: She needs the Lord, Mavis . . .

MAVIS: I know she does. Somethin' tells me she knows it too. That's what I been prayin' for anyhow. Well, I just hope she finds happiness in her marriage . . .

HENRY: Just like we did?

MAVIS: Uh-huh. Henry, you remember our weddin' day?

HENRY: Yeah, I do. I was s' nervous, thought I was gonna pass out . . . but then . . . I got to the altar . . . turned around and looked up that aisle . . . and there you were . . . perty as a pi'ture. I really thought I was gonna pass out then!

MAVIS: Oh you!

HENRY: Mavis, are you really happy? I mean, we've stayed right here in Pondtown all our lives. Never been nowheres much . . .

MAVIS: Now, we've taken some trips from time to time. Went down to the Azalea Trail a couple a times. Remember that time we went to Atlanta to see your sister? That was nice.

HENRY: Oooo, I won't never go back. Them big four-lane highways up there . . . cars flyin' by . . . I was a nervous wreck. I remember the time we took a trip up to that lake, can't remember the name of it now, but it was a real pretty lake somewheres up in Kentucky.

MAVIS: Kentucky lake?

HENRY: Yeah, that was it. Kentucky Lake. *(Takes her hand)* Mavis? Are you happy?

MAVIS: How could I not be happy? I'm married to a finest gentleman ever created. I have lots of friends and family who love me, and I'm doin' exactly what God wants me to do. That's what happiness is, knowin' you're doin' right for the Lord's sake.

HENRY: You still got His smile in your heart, Mavis.

MAVIS: What?

HENRY: You know, that's what first attracted me to you. I'd look over at you settin' there on the pew next to your mama. You was just a girl but awful perty even then, but more than that you had the Lord's smile. Yep, still perty—still got His smile.

MAVIS: Oh . . .

(Enter GENEVA *at front door.)*

GENEVA: All right. Break it up, you two. It's *my* wedding day. Not yours!

HENRY: Why, Geneva, you're early. You already ready to go to the church?

GENEVA: Not yet . . .

MAVIS: Oh, don't you look perty, Geneva. A beautiful bride.

GENEVA: Yeah, well . . . I've got a lot of experience being a bride.

MAVIS: We're just so happy for you, Geneva. We're prayin' that the Lord'll bless this marriage for eternity.

GENEVA: Or 'til *Charlie's* death do us part?

HENRY: What?

GENEVA: I'm sorry. I shouldn't have said that. I'm just afraid that . . . well, I hope Charlie and I can be as happy as you two.

HENRY: Hey, ladies, I'll go out and get some more rice. I'll be back directly. *(Exits front door)*

GENEVA: Mavis, you know I kept waiting for you to hate me.

MAVIS: Why, Geneva. I never hated you . . .

GENEVA: I know. That's just it. When I came here I thought everybody hated me. My mother-in-law sure did. I thought the town did too—and God. I kept expecting you to—but you never did.

MAVIS: No, never.

GENEVA: Hated myself enough for both of us. I passed on some of that hate to my boys, too, I suppose. Hope they'll forgive me one day.

MAVIS: You've had a lot a pain in your life, Geneva.

GENEVA: But, Mavis, you've had pain in your life too. You've lost your mother, your father, both of your brothers. You didn't even see your sister, Mattie, for years. But still, you loved people, you loved me. I'll never forget that. You know, it was because of you that I'm getting married today.

MAVIS: Oh, now, what do you mean, Geneva? I didn't even know Charlie until you introduced me to him.

GENEVA: Mavis, after Tuck died I swore I'd never love again. I married Althus, you know, 'cause I was poor and scared and alone. But in my way, I tried to love him. After he died, there I was swearing again I'd never find love. But you showed me that somebody in this world could love me in spite of everything. *(Pause)* Mavis, you've shown me something else.

MAVIS: What's that?

GENEVA: Well, I told Henry when I first moved here that I wasn't very religious. What I meant was that I didn't even know if there was a God. I'd never seen Him, I'd never heard Him. . . . Then for 30 years I watched you, listened to you, observed your life. Mavis, you not only showed me there was a God . . . but you showed me what He's like.

(Characters onstage freeze and stage lights dim a bit. Light up on STORYTELLER.*)*

STORYTELLER: The wedding was real perty. Geneva looked happy for the first time in her life.

Ever'body was there. Me and Waylon, Sammy Dale—and Reveline. Mavis cried a course. Henry look almost fatherly even though he was giving away a bride that was his own age. We had the reception down at the café. Ever'body seemed to have a real good time.

We sent the happy couple off on their honeymoon in high style. Waylon escorted their Datsun to the county line with the siren a-blastin'.

(Enter WAYLON, REVELINE, SAMMY DALE, MAVIS, HENRY *at front door.)*

WAYLON: OK, Reveline. Now what?

REVELINE: Waylon, have you seen that smoke comin' outta the stack at the Heil plant?

WAYLON: Yes, I have.

REVELINE: Well . . . they got laws against that, don't they?

WAYLON: Yeah, but they've already been checked out by the federal government . . . and they're meetin' standards.

REVELINE: Well, how do you explain those mysterious deaths?

WAYLON: What mysterious deaths?

REVELINE: Well, Ralph Beevis, for instance.

SAMMY DALE: Ralph Beevis was 95 years old.

REVELINE: But he was healthy as a horse . . .

WAYLON *(interrupting):* He was healthy 'til he died, Reveline.

SAMMY DALE: What do you think, Henry?

HENRY: Huh? 'Bout what?

WAYLON: 'Bout Ralph Beevis dyin' . . .

(Men mime conversation during onstage lights dim to blackout. Light up on STORYTELLER. *Music begins under and continues under the following and through blackout.)*

STORYTELLER: Folks were always askin' Henry his opinion on ever'thing from life to death . . . on account a Henry was wise, kinda like Solomon. 'Course Solomon was rich and lived in a big old palace. Henry and Mavis just lived in a clapboard house down on Main, right next to the café.

(Blackout)

Scene 5

Time: Anytime.

(As light comes up on STORYTELLER, *music fades out. Sound effect: telephone rings.)*

STORYTELLER: I knew it was bad news soon as the phone rang. Ya know how ya just know? Wasn't too surprised though. Henry had been lookin' sort a poorly for a while—kinda holler-eyed. Doc said it was his heart. Said Henry needed to go to Birmingham to that big hospital and get some tests run. Mavis tried to get him to but . . . well, he kept puttin' her off. I'd see Mavis back in the kitchen, her brow furrowed, her lips movin'. I knew she was talkin' to the Lord 'bout it. Then I'd see that peaceful look on her face, like the Lord was talkin' back.

(Lights up dimly on café scene. There is a funeral spray on an easel by the front door.)

Then Henry was gone. Mavis said he died just like he lived—sure a where he was goin'.

I can't explain it. At the funeral, we all cried and cried, but there was somethin' 'sides mournin' goin' on. The church house was overflowin' with friends and family . . . and on ever' face, I could see what Henry Love was put on this earth for.

(Lights up onstage right where WAYLON, SAMMY DALE, WENDELL, JR., *and* STRANGER *are discovered.)*

WAYLON: It was after midnight, if I recollect. I was wore out, but I couldn't sleep. Had too much on my mind. Devil was after me somethin' fierce. I'd just been swore in as sheriff and the very next day I was offered a whole bunch a money to look the other way while's a crime was goin' on. I can't tell you how tempted I was. It woulda been the easiest money I ever made. Went out for a walk that night and ended up on Main, right in front a Henry's. There he was settin' on his front porch like he was waitin' for me. When I told him why I was so stirred, he knew exactly what to say: "Waylon," he said, "God gave us laws to help us know our limits. He gave us grace to live inside 'em."

SAMMY DALE: Henry always said I was a good salesman. He'd buy what I had to sell from time to time. He probably had the largest collection a Fuller Brushes in this county. One time when we was just settin' around talking he says to me, "Sammy Dale, you could sell just about anything, but there's one thing you won't never have to sell. The gospel." He says, "Gospel's like a lion in a cage. You don't have to defend it or nothin'. All you have to do is open up the door and let it out. It'll take care of itself."

WENDELL, JR. *(reading from letter):* "Dear Wendell, Mavis and me want you to know that we're prayin' for ya and that we're takin' care a your mama, too, 'til you see fit to come home. But 'til then, next time you see a nice big open field somewhere where's there's lots a wildflowers, go set right in the middle of it and remember, that's how our love for you grows—wild, plentiful, and surrounding you always. Your friend, Henry Love."

STRANGER: I offered him $50,000 for the café. That was maybe twice what it was worth. But Henry Love turned me down. Said, "Some folks think they're worth a lot a money just 'cause they have it."

(Lights down onstage right. Light up on STORYTELLER.*)*

STORYTELLER: Mavis decided to keep the place open for the time bein'. It was hard for her . . . well, it was hard for all of us. Not seein' Henry there in his usual place, perty near broke our hearts. But we all helped out, on account a ever'body had been touched by the lives of Henry and Mavis Love.

And then, one mornin', Mavis didn't show up to open the café, and again, we all knew, and we were right. Mavis had gone to be with the Lord, just like Henry. She was gone—finally home. And then ever'body had a chance to look back again, and ever'body realized they had a little dab a Mavis's godly smile in their hearts too.

(Lights up onstage left where we discover REVELINE, CHRISTINE, GENEVA, *and* MATTIE.*)*

REVELINE: She was always the first to help out. In my work, I'd see babies who were undernourished and old folks whose houses were cold and drafty. Oh, the county had funds to help feed and tend to these folks, but seems like Mavis was always there to add the extra comforts that our provisions couldn't supply.

CHRISTINE: I thought she was an angel. Hers was the first face I saw when I woke up in the hospital. Accordin' to the nurses, Mavis brought me in after I got so sick, I couldn't hardly breathe. I had the pneumonia and 'bout died. Probably would have if Mavis hadn't been there to make me eat and take care a me.

GENEVA: I had nobody in the world who cared about me. No family. No friends. I remember after the twins were born and Missus Tucker asked us to leave. Mavis and Henry let us stay in their home until we could find a place of our own. They helped me find a job. Mavis would even watch the boys for me while I went to beauty school.

MATTIE: Ever since we were little girls, Mavis had a tender heart. She was always helping people—always caring—always leavin' behind a trail of kindness.

(Lights dim as characters exit.)

STORYTELLER: For the first time in over 40 years, Love's Café was closed for business. Henry and Mavis had left most a their worldly goods to Mattie, but as usual they didn't forgit 'bout old Christine. They made sure that I had a little somethin' to retire on and a little extra to take a nice bus trip up to Canada.

(MATTIE *enters café scene from kitchen and removes funeral spray. She dusts a bit, then exits.)* Some feller from Atlanta tried to buy the place from Mattie and put in a Laundromat, but Mattie figured that the café could do a lot more for folks in Pondtown than clean up their laundry. It had always been a place where folks could go and find good food, good fellowship, and the love of God served up in style. So Mattie waited and prayed 'til a young couple came along and wanted to buy the place and open it again as a café. The couple happened to be James, Mattie's oldest boy, and his new bride.

(Enter JAMES *and* SANDRA *at front door. They survey the café.)*

See, the influence of Henry and Mavis Love reached farther than the city limits a Pondtown. It had trickled out into the hearts a folks who then would pass it on to somebody else. James told his wife, Sandra, how he'd go down and visit each summer with his Uncle Henry and Aunt Mavis and how he first heard the gospel.

Not only did James learn the secret of Mavis's delicious cornbread, he also learned about the love a God . . . back in the kitchen at Love's Café.

JAMES: Well, Sandra, what do you think? Think we're ready to open the doors?

SANDRA: I guess I'm as ready as I'll ever be.

(Blackout)

PERFORMANCE LICENSING AGREEMENT

Lillenas Drama Resources
Performance Licensing
P.O. Box 419527, Kansas City, MO 64141

Name ____

Organization ____

Address ____

City ______________________ State ______ ZIP __________

Play ____

Number of performances intended ______________________

Approximate dates ____________________________________

Amount remitted* $____________

Mail to Lillenas at the address above

Order performance copies of this script from your local bookstore or directly from the publisher.

*$15.00 for the first performance; $10.00 each subsequent performance

PERFORMANCE LICENSING AGREEMENT

Lillenas Drama Resources
Performance Licensing
P.O. Box 419527, Kansas City, MO 64141

Name ____

Organization ______________________________________

Address ____

City ______________________ State ______ ZIP ________

Play ____

Number of performances intended ____________________

Approximate dates __________________________________

Amount remitted* $____________

Mail to Lillenas at the address above

Order performance copies of this script from your local bookstore or directly from the publisher.

*$15.00 for the first performance; $10.00 each subsequent performance